something to
CELEBRATE

something to CELEBRATE

ann baber

MEREHURST

contents

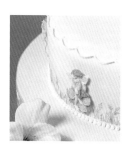

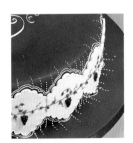

This book is dedicated to my sister Linda Rutter

introduction

The decoration of both wedding and celebration cakes has progressed with incredible rapidity in the last twenty years. Probably more new ideas, equipment and design techniques have appeared since the 1980s than in the previous hundred or so, when Queen Victoria gave the royal-iced wedding cake her seal of approval. The business of transforming a piece of fruit cake or sponge into a beautiful cake has now become a modern art form. The skills required range from basic to those that need a great deal of practice and knowledge, as well as a very steady hand.

One of the great joys of this new-found freedom of cake decorating is the thriving enthusiasm of cake decorators on a global scale. Today, one can travel to almost any corner of the world and encounter dedicated and talented cake decorators, all ready to share their skills – hence the exciting cross-pollination of so many new ideas.

To be asked to contribute via a book to this ever-growing versatile craft is indeed not only a pleasure but also a challenge – the challenge being to provide fellow cake decorators with ideas considered to be worth exploring, expanding and adapting until, with love, skill and patience, they produce a cake of which they are truly proud.

Ann Baker

fabric effects

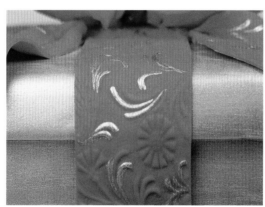

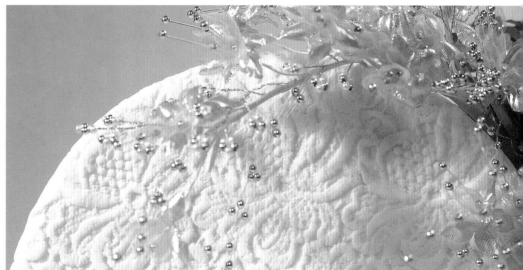

all about fabric effects

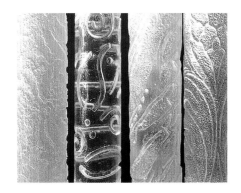

Create different fabric effects by using a variety of embossed rolling pins.

Roll sugarpaste with embossed pins to give a cake the look of embroidered cloth.

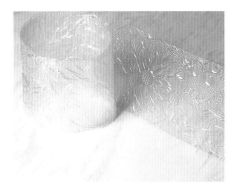

Embossed plastic wraps are now available in a number of different designs.

Fabric effects are an integral part of modern cake decorating. They range from simple techniques such as wrapping a strip of sugarpaste (rolled fondant) around a cake to represent a ribbon, to more complicated effects such as draping swathes of sugarpaste down a tiered cake. Very little piping is required when using fabric effects and, since the base covering can be completed very quickly, this leaves more time for experimenting with other forms of decoration.

Fabric effects can be greatly enhanced by embossing the sugarpaste. Work as quickly as possible in order to prevent any cracking in the surface of the paste. The longer you leave sugarpaste after it has been rolled, the more likely it is to dry out and crack. The best draping effects are achieved using sugarpaste that has a certain elasticity, which allows stretching without breaking. If in doubt, mix sugarpaste with either gelatine paste or flowerpaste (see pages 111–12) in a 50:50 ratio.

EMBOSSED ROLLING PINS

With the advent of long (36cm/14in, 41cm/16in and 51cm/20in) embossed rolling pins, you can now roll out and emboss a piece of sugarpaste large enough to cover a whole cake in one go. The finished cake takes on the appearance of embroidered cloth, and additional enhancement can be achieved by picking out features of the design with colour.

To emboss a piece of sugarpaste, dust the underside evenly with icing (powdered) sugar to keep it from sticking to the tabletop. Roll out the paste to about a 5mm (1/4in) thickness using an ordinary rolling pin (this allows for additional thinning of the paste by the pressure of the textured rolling pin). Roll the textured rolling pin firmly over the sugarpaste. Pick up large embossed pieces of sugarpaste with a plain rolling pin rather than your hands: do not use the textured pin, as the weight of the paste on the pin may distort the original pattern.

EMBOSSED PLASTIC WRAPS

Embossed strips of plastic, 84cm (33in) long, 8cm (31/4in) wide and sufficient to wrap around a 25cm (10in) cake, are now readily available in several different designs. It is not necessary to grease the wrap before use, or even to dust it with icing sugar, as long as it is spotlessly clean. The best way to store plastic wrap is by hanging it up rather than rolling it, or by keeping it flat if you have room.

Wraps can be used to emboss sugarpaste, marzipan and chocolate. When using plastic wrap with sugarpaste, lay the wrap concave-side-down on a strip of sugarpaste. Press hard with a rolling pin to imprint the pattern of the wrap onto the paste, then trim. To apply the strip to the cake, carefully roll it up like a bandage. Lightly brush the sides of the cake with boiled water (or royal icing for an iced cake), then unwrap the rolled strip of sugarpaste around the sides of the cake. The imprinted strips can also be made into bows, draped down the length of a stacked cake or applied as panels of decoration.

If you wish to emboss a cake covered with a different medium such as chocolate, wrap the coated plastic around the cake while it is still soft but not runny, then allow it to set in the refrigerator. When you peel off the wrap, you will be left with a chocolate 'ribbon' around the cake in the exact pattern of the wrap.

ALTERNATIVE EQUIPMENT FOR EMBOSSING

If you wish to experiment with fabric effects but do not have an embossed rolling pin or patterned plastic wrap, try using some of the following items.

Heavily embossed wallpaper Most home decorating stores are happy to provide sample pieces of paper free of charge, and there are many different designs to choose from. Use in the same way as plastic wrap.

String Tie string in a random pattern around a plain rolling pin and experiment by rolling it over the sugarpaste in several directions.

Lace You can emboss the pattern from one or more pieces of lace onto sugarpaste. Choose thick lace with a smooth surface so that cotton fibres do not stick to the surface of the cake, and apply the pattern in the same way as plastic wrap.

Plastic doilies These are good for embossing sugarpaste that is to be laid over the top of the cake like a tablecloth. Again, use it in the same way as plastic wrap.

Try embossing with a plastic open-weave bag or string wrapped around a pin.

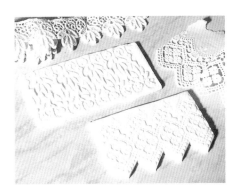

Cotton lace can also be pressed into sugarpaste for fine and intricate designs.

Heavily designed wallpaper with raised patterns is also good for embossing.

pink and silver celebration

This simple cake will suit beginner cake decorators as it requires very little piping – the pin creates most of the design. Enhanced by the highly textured surface created by long-length embossed rolling pins, this sumptuous creation offers plenty of scope for a full and elaborate floral bouquet, in either silk or sugar.

CAKE AND DECORATION

- 25cm (10in) and 20cm (8in) round fruit cakes
- 3kg (6lb) marzipan
- 33cm (13in) round cake board
- 3.25kg (6lb 8oz) pink sugarpaste (rolled fondant)
- Icing (powdered) sugar
- 250g (8oz) pink or white royal icing
- Silver flowers and leaves

ESSENTIAL EQUIPMENT

- Embossed rolling pin (Rosgar AB) or see page 11 for alternatives
- Piece of foam or couple of tea (kitchen) towels
- No.2 piping tube (tip)
- Greaseproof (parchment) paper piping bags (cones)
- Posy pick

1 Marzipan the 25cm (10in) cake and set aside for 4 to 5 days.

2 Cut 3.5cm (1¼in) off the second cake, leaving neat, flat edges (see page 115). Marzipan the top and sides first, then leave for a further 4 to 5 days.

3 Cover the cake board with the pink sugarpaste (rolled fondant) at the same time as covering the cake. Alternatively, leave the board plain and cover it separately. Place the cake on the board when it is dry enough to handle.

4 Lightly dust a flat, clean surface with icing (powdered) sugar and roll out the sugarpaste to a 5mm (¼in) thickness – ensure you roll out enough paste to cover the entire cake. When rolling out large amounts of sugarpaste, keep the paste in motion and frequently dust your working area with a little icing sugar to prevent the paste from sticking. Do not use too much icing sugar as this will dry the paste, making it unmanageable. Never use cornflour (cornstarch) as it absorbs moisture very quickly and will cause the paste to dry and crack fast.

5 Using an embossed pin, firmly roll over the sugarpaste, making sure the full texture of the design is clear all over the paste. You can go back and re-roll small sections if the pattern is not clear without spoiling.

First roll out the sugarpaste with a normal pin, then roll firmly with the textured pin.

Lift the embossed paste onto the cake with a plain rolling pin.

Take the sugarpaste to the edge of the board as an alternative way of covering.

Marzipan both front and back of the top cake before covering with sugarpaste.

Use a paper template to cut the correct shape of marzipan for the top cake.

6 Lightly brush the marzipanned surface of the 25cm (10in) cake with boiled water. Lift up the embossed paste with a plain rolling pin and cover the cake, taking care not to press too hard on the paste as this may cause some of the design to be lost. Leave the paste to dry on a spare cake board or tray, then place the cake onto the sugarpasted cake board.

7 Place the 20cm (8in) cake onto a sheet of paper, then draw and cut out around the shape. Place the cake on a clean piece of foam or a couple of folded tea (kitchen) towels. Roll out some more marzipan, place the paper shape onto it and cut around. Brush some boiled apricot jam onto the surface of the cake, lay the marzipan on top and smooth into place either with a smoother or the surface of your hand. Gently pinch the edges of the marzipan to eliminate any gaps, and smooth over with the centre of your hand. Turn the cake over and repeat on the remaining uncovered side. Allow to dry for 1 to 2 days.

8 Cover the top and sides of the 20cm (8in) cake with a piece of embossed sugarpaste, then cover the back and front of the cake using the same technique as for the marzipan. Brush a little boiled water onto the larger cake in the area where the smaller one will sit. Place the smaller cake upright onto the larger.

9 Fit a piping bag (cone) with a no.2 icing tube (tip) and fill it with either pink or white royal icing. Pipe some small pearls around the cake. Make sure you situate the join at the back of the cake so that it does not look unsightly. Then, pipe some larger pearls around the base of both cakes.

10 Attach the spray to the top of the structure using a posy pick. Secure the posy pick with either a small amount of royal icing or some extra sugarpaste and a little boiled water. Feel free to use your own choice of spray, depending on the flowers and foliage available.

sugarcraft tips

• If using a more unconventional embossing medium – covered rolling pin or wallpaper for instance (see page 11) – it is preferable to practise on some spare sugarpaste first.

• Pick up larger pieces of sugarpaste with a rolling pin rather than using your hands, to prevent tearing.

pearl wedding cake

Many brides wear pearls either in their hair or on their dress. Therefore, I thought it would be an attractive idea to have a cake that is almost totally devoted to pearls. In this particular creation, the use of feathers beautifully complements the delicacy of the pearl decoration.

CAKE AND DECORATION
- 25cm (10in), 20cm (8in) and 15cm (6in) round, rich fruit cakes, 10cm (4in) deep
- 4kg (8lb) marzipan
- 36cm (14in) round cake board
- 20cm (8in) and 15cm (6in) round, thin cake boards
- 5kg (10lb) sugarpaste (rolled fondant)
- White satin dusting powder (petal dust) (EA)
- 250g (8oz) royal icing
- 3.5m (11ft) rope of pearls of two different sizes (half and half)
- Selection of pearl sprays, leaves and feathers

ESSENTIAL EQUIPMENT
- Embossed plastic wrap (AB) or see page 11 for alternatives
- Small, sharp knife
- Veining tool
- Large, soft-bristled paintbrush
- Greaseproof (parchment) paper piping bags (cones)
- White floristry tape

1 Marzipan all three cakes. Leave to harden for at least 5 days.

2 Coat the 36cm (14in) cake board with sugarpaste (rolled fondant). Slip the two round, thin cake boards under the middle and top tier cakes.

3 Coat all three cakes with sugarpaste and leave to harden for 2 to 4 days.

4 Put the largest cake board on a small board, and transfer them to a tray that is larger than the cake board so that the cake can be transported more easily.

5 Roll out some sugarpaste to the length and width of the plastic wrap, and about 2.5mm (1/8in) thick. Place the wrap, concave-side-down, onto the paste. Press down with your hands, then roll quite hard with a rolling pin. Trim the paste to the shape of the wrap with a sharp knife, then peel off the wrap. As the cakes become smaller, measure the cakes, then trim the sugarpaste to the correct size. Use a veining tool to emphasize the leaf design if you wish. Generously brush the surface of the embossed strip of sugarpaste with white satin dusting powder (petal dust), then roll it up like a bandage and stand upright.

6 Lightly brush the sides of the largest cake with some boiled water. Starting at what will be the back of the cake, unwrap the embossed sugarpaste strip

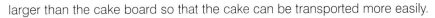

Use plastic wrap with a leaf pattern to decorate the sides of the cake.

Create strips of embossed sugarpaste by firmly rolling the plastic wrap onto them.

Emphasize the leaf design by outlining the pattern with a veining tool.

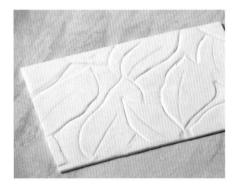

Apply more pressure around the edges of the leaves and less onto the veins within.

Brush the embossed strips with dusting powder before applying them to the cake.

around the edges of the cake. Trim off any overlap where the two ends meet with a sharp knife. Gently smooth the edges with a ball tool.

7 Fill a piping bag (cone) with royal icing, no tube (tip) necessary. Pipe a thin line of icing around the base of the embossed strip and fasten the rope of larger pearls. Repeat this process at the top of the strip, using the smaller pearls. Place the next tier of cake in place and repeat the process, and once again with the top tier. If desired, add extra piping in the space between the top of each strip and the next cake.

8 Make several small sprays of the pearls, leaves and feathers, binding them together with white floristry tape. Arrange this top decoration, and fix it to the cake in either a posy pick or with a little sugarpaste secured to the surface of the cake.

sugarcraft tips

• Dowelling is optional if using rich fruit cake (see page 110), particularly if the cakes have been allowed to dry thoroughly between the coatings of marzipan and sugarpaste.

• After brushing white satin powder onto the sugarpaste strip, give it an extra glow by briskly brushing or burnishing with a clean brush.

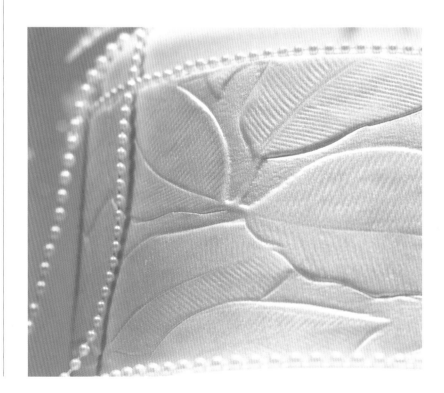

lemon daisies

This stunning creation offers a pleasing combination of two techniques: the popular brush embroidery and a coloured, embossed panel of sugarpaste, set alternately around a hexagonal cake. Sugarcraft beginners could use all-embossed panels, with the choice of varying the colours of the daisies.

CAKE AND DECORATION

- 7.5cm (3in) thin cake board
- 4kg (8lb) sugarpaste (rolled fondant)
- 30cm (12in) hexagonal fruit cake, 9cm (3¹/₂in) deep
- 3kg (6lb) marzipan
- 41cm (16in) and 36cm (14in) cake boards
- 500g (1lb) royal icing
- Lemon and moss green dusting powders (petal dusts)
- 1.5m (2yd) x 1cm (¹/₂in) lemon or white ribbon
- Silk or sugar daisies with leaves

ESSENTIAL EQUIPMENT

- Glass panel (optional)
- Greaseproof (parchment) paper piping bags (cones)
- Nos.1 and 2 piping tubes (tips)
- Scribing tool
- 2 small bowls
- Paintbrushes
- Embossed plastic wrap (A) or see page 11 for alternatives

1 In advance, cover the small, thin cake board with sugarpaste (rolled fondant), then place a small mound of sugarpaste in the centre of the board to support the floral arrangement.

2 Marzipan the cake, then transfer it to a spare cake board or a clean tray. Allow to dry for 4 to 5 days.

3 For the brush-embroidered panels, trace out the design onto tracing paper

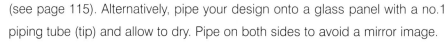

(see page 115). Alternatively, pipe your design onto a glass panel with a no.1 piping tube (tip) and allow to dry. Pipe on both sides to avoid a mirror image.

4 Stick the two cake boards together and cover them with sugarpaste.

5 Coat the cake with sugarpaste. If you are using a design piped onto glass, press it onto the side of the cake while it is still soft. As you are pressing on the glass, hold a smoother flat to the opposite side of the cake, which will prevent fingermarks from appearing when pressing firmly, to obtain a good, clear outline.

6 If inscribing the pattern, wait until the cake has hardened up a little. Some people will have no problem simply brush icing freehand, not needing the use of a pattern at all.

For the top decoration, cover a small, thin cake board with sugarpaste.

The mound of sugarpaste in the centre of the board will support the arrangement.

Inscribe the design you wish to brush ice onto slightly hardened sugarpaste.

Use a fine paintbrush to work the colour from the outer edges into the centre.

Create the brush icing using a paintbrush and some soft royal icing.

7 Place the cake onto the sugarpasted board. Using royal icing, pipe some pearls around the base of the cake. Allow them to dry thoroughly, as they will help to hold the cake in place when it is being worked on.

8 Put about a tablespoon of royal icing into two separate bowls and colour one lemon and the other green. Add the colour with a cocktail stick (toothpick) until you reach the required shade. Then, slowly add small quantities of water, stirring after each addition, until the icing becomes a thick cream consistency.

9 Insert the coloured icings into two separate piping bags (cones), no tubes necessary. Tilt the cake to the appropriate angle, then cut a hole at the end of the bag containing the lemon icing. The hole should be approximately the size of a no.1 tube. Do not cut the green bag until you are ready to use it, as the icing will dry out since there is no tube.

10 Working one petal or leaf at a time, pipe a thick line of icing at the top of the petal/leaf. Then, gradually thin out the line towards the base of the petal/leaf by applying less pressure on the bag. Using the point of a paintbrush, pull the icing downwards from the lower edge of the icing, leaving the outer edge of the petal/leaf untouched and looking plump. As you are pulling the lines of icing down, make sure that they curve towards the centre on both sides of the petal/leaf. Ensure that the icing is thinner at the base of the petal/leaf. Allow the icing to dry, then dust a little more colour onto the petals/leaves to highlight.

11 For the embossed panels, roll out some sugarpaste the length and width of the plastic wrap. Place the wrap concave-side-down onto the

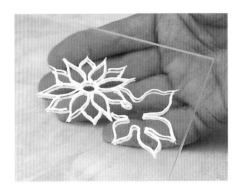

Alternatively, pipe the chosen design onto both sides of a glass panel.

paste and roll over firmly with a pin. Trim, cut to the panel size and repeat the process three times. Allow the panels to dry for about 2 to 3 days so they are easier to handle, then dust in the food colourings. To paint the stems, mix the dusting powder (petal dust) with a little water in order to obtain finer lines. Spread a small amount of royal icing onto the back of the panel and carefully attach the pieces of embossed paste to the cake.

12 To finish off the decorative panels, pipe a series of very small pearls around the edge of the sugarpaste. If desired, you can add a touch of freehand embroidery to the brush-iced panel.

13 Attach your choice of ribbon – lemon or white – to the edge of the cake board, then arrange the top decoration of silk or sugar flowers and leaves.

Press the design onto the side of the cake while the sugarpaste is still soft.

sugarcraft tips

• If you mix a powder food colouring with alcohol, it will quickly revert back to powder because alcohol evaporates fast, unlike water.

• When brush icing on the side of a cake, make sure that the icing is not mixed with too much water. If it becomes too thin, it will start to run down the side of the cake. Practise on the side of a cake tin or a basin first until you obtain the correct consistency.

• For more information on piping to enhance the finished panels, see page 32.

Once the embossed panels are dry, dust more colour onto the design as highlights.

christmas parcel

Nowadays, few people have time to decorate an elaborate Christmas cake. This parcel cake may look rather sophisticated but, by making the bows in advance, you will find this cake is easier to achieve than expected. Arrange small presents around the base of the cake to enhance the Christmas theme and appeal to children.

CAKE AND DECORATION

- 23cm (9in) square, rich fruit cake, 10cm (4in) deep
- 2kg (4lb) marzipan
- 3kg (6lb) sugarpaste (rolled fondant)
- Christmas red paste food colouring
- Rose gold dusting powder (petal dust) (EA)
- Painting solution (EA)
- 36cm (14in) square black cake board

ESSENTIAL EQUIPMENT

- Embossed plastic wrap (AB) or see page 11 for alternatives
- Small, sharp knife
- Cardboard tubing or rolling pin
- Plate or tile
- 2 large soft bristle paintbrushes
- Smaller paintbrush
- Foam pieces for support

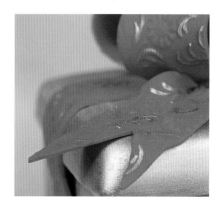

1 Marzipan the cake and leave to dry on a spare board for 3 to 4 days.

2 Colour about 500g (1lb) of the sugarpaste (rolled fondant) red and store it in a plastic bag until needed.

3 Cover the cake with white sugarpaste, making sure the paste goes right to the bottom edge of the cake. Trim the paste, ensuring that there are no gaps visible as there will not be any piping around the base. Place the cake on a spare board and leave to dry for at least 4 days.

4 To make the loops for the bow, roll a strip of the red sugarpaste, emboss it with wrap and cut to a width of 6.5cm (2¹/₂in). Cut pieces 18cm (7in) long and cut each end into a 'V' shape. With a small paintbrush, dab the non-embossed side of the strip with a little boiled water. Press both ends together at the 'V' point and upwards for about 1.5cm (¹/₂in). Place the strip on cardboard tubing or a rolling pin to dry. If the base of the bow looks uneven, neaten by cutting with scissors. Make at least six bows, more if you wish. Also cut two ribbon ends by measuring two lengths of the embossed strip, one 13cm (5in) long and the other a little shorter. Cut an inverted 'V' and place it on a spare board in a slightly twisted angle to give a realistic appearance. Leave to dry.

Paint rose gold dust mixed with painting solution over the entire sugarpasted cake.

Place a plastic wrap or some embossed paper onto a rolled strip of red paste.

Press with a rolling pin to transfer the pattern from the wrap to the sugarpaste.

Cut 6.5cm (2¹/₂in) wide strips of embossed paste to make the bow loops.

Form the loops of the bow by wrapping the strips around a cardboard tube.

5 Roll out the remainder of the white sugarpaste into a 31cm (12¹/₄in) square and place it onto the cake for the lid. Do not secure it at this stage as you might need to move the paste around a little to get it level. Once it is level, lift the paste here and there and brush lightly with some boiled water for adherence. Smooth the top of the square and, if necessary, trim what is now the bottom edge of the lid so it is perfectly straight. Allow to set for at least a day.

6 On a plate or tile, mix some rose gold dust with painting solution until you reach a soft paste consistency. With a large brush, paint the entire cake with long, even strokes until it is completely covered. Leave the cake to dry thoroughly. Burnish any streaks with a clean, dry brush.

7 To avoid finger marks on the gold surface, lift the cake by sliding a large palette knife under it and holding the cake at a sufficient angle for your hand to slip under. With both your hand and the knife, transfer the cake to the black board. Remove your hand, then lower the cake onto the board with the knife.

8 Measure the cake from the base, over the top and down to the opposite base. Roll some more red sugarpaste and cut two strips 6.5cm (2¹/₂in) wide, and fractionally longer than required. Place them

crosswise over the cake. Lift the cake with the palette knife and tuck the surplus ribbon under all four sides of the cake to give the appearance that the ribbon is going all the way around it.

9 Use a fine paintbrush to pick out highlights in the bow loops with gold. Leave to dry thoroughly, then attach the dry bows to the top of the cake with some red sugarpaste softened with a little water. Prop the bows in place with pieces of foam. Finally, slot in the ribbon ends.

sugarcraft tips

- Try painting the cake in other dark colours, such as holly green, black or navy blue. Decorate the parcel with a gold sugar ribbon.
- Do not worry about covering a cake of this size with the edible gold dust – it is perfectly safe.
- If using one of the softer sugarpastes, use equal quantities of flowerpaste when making the bows. Alternatively, add half a teaspoon of gum tragacanth to the paste in order for the bows to become hard enough to hold their shape.

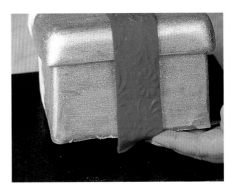

Tuck strips of sugarpaste ribbon under the cake as if wrapped around it.

Pick out highlights of the embossed design on the bow loops with gold.

Highlight the ribbon ends with gold and allow to dry before putting them in place.

white and gold drape

My sister gave me the idea for this cake while we were travelling together. Originally, the drape was to be sectioned by a gold, gelatine-paste hair clip, but these sections would have needed to be proportioned very precisely. The ties featured here are equally attractive, easier to make and much less time consuming.

CAKE AND DECORATION
- 30cm (12in), 25cm (10in), 20cm (8in) and 15cm (6in) round fruit cakes, 10cm (4in) deep
- 5kg (10lb) marzipan
- 41cm (16in) round cake board
- 6.5kg (13^{1}/4lb) white sugarpaste (rolled fondant)
- 25cm (10in), 20cm (8in) and 15cm (6in) round, thin cake boards
- Bright gold edible metallic dusting powder (petal dust) (EA)
- Painting solution (EA)
- White shortening (optional)
- 2 large gold gerberas
- Gold foliage
- 1.5m (2yd) x 1cm (1/2in) white ribbon
- 1.5m (2yd) x 5mm (1/4in) gold ribbon

ESSENTIAL EQUIPMENT
- Embossed plastic wrap (AB) or see page 11 for alternatives
- Sharp knife
- Smallest of set of 3 scallop cutters (AB) (optional)
- Polystyrene chips or foam sponge
- No.4 paintbrush
- Clay gun (using the largest of the three multi-holed discs)

1 Cover all four cakes with marzipan, then allow them to dry for a minimum of 5 days.

2 Cover the cakes as well as the 41cm (16in) cake board with sugarpaste (rolled fondant). Slip the thin cake boards under the three smaller cakes. Then, dowel the bottom, second and third tiers with plastic dowels while the sugarpaste is still soft (see page 110). Leave to dry for at least 4 days.

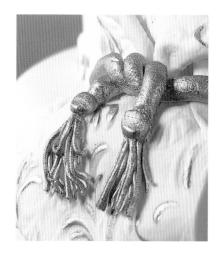

3 Stack the cakes by placing them almost level at the back of the main board. This will leave approximately 3.5cm (1^{1}/4in) at the front of each cake – except the base cake, which is to be placed in the centre of the board.

4 Roll out some more sugarpaste thinly to the length and width of the plastic wrap. Place the wrap concave-side-down onto the sugarpaste and, with a rolling pin, roll very firmly over the top of the wrap, impressing the design into the paste. Cut strips of paste 1cm (1/2in) wide. Lightly brush some boiled water onto the cakes where the strips are to be attached. Attach the strips around the bases of the cakes, ensuring that the joins in the strips are at the back of the cakes for aesthetic purposes.

Use a rolling pin to transfer the pattern from the wrap onto the sugarpaste drape.

Cut narrow strips of sugarpaste to wrap around the base of each cake.

Drape the wide embossed strip of sugarpaste down the tiers of the cake.

Pinch in the drape at the base of each cake with your fingers.

Lay some polystyrene chips here and there under the drape for movement.

5 You will need to place the front drape onto the cake in two pieces for convenience. Take two measurements, one from the middle of the top tier to the base of the second tier, and the other from the base of the second tier to the edge of the baseboard. Roll out more sugarpaste quite thinly and emboss it (see step 4). Cut the first measured length, pinch one end in quite tightly and place it in the centre of the top tier. Secure the paste with some boiled water. Flow the rest of the paste down the centre of the cake until you reach the first 'shelf' at the base of the top tier. Pinch the paste, secure it with a little boiled water and flow the remaining paste down to the base of the second tier.

6 Repeat the above for the other tiers, allowing the paste to flow down to the edge of the cake board. If desired, trim off the end of the drape with a small scallop cutter. Pinch in the drape on each tier, then place some polystyrene chips randomly under the drape to add movement.

7 Mix some bright gold dusting powder (petal dust) with painting solution. Then, paint in the highlights of the pattern – on the drape as well as on the sugarpaste 'ribbons' around the bases of the cakes.

8 Roll out eight sugarpaste strips the thickness of your little finger and 15cm (6in) long. Cross two pieces over to form a half-knot, leaving a 2.5cm (1in) 'tail'. Secure the knots to the drape with a little boiled water, then trim. Repeat on the other cakes.

9 Lightly grease the inside of the clay gun with a little white shortening (this is optional but it does make the job easier). Add a very small amount of water to some sugarpaste in order to soften it slightly. Roll the paste into a fine strip and push it down into the gun. Push down the handle of the gun and squeeze out about 4cm (1¹/₂in) of paste. Cut off the paste with a sharp knife and place it onto a flat surface. Repeat this eight times.

10 Separate strands of tassel with the tip of the knife and join the tassels to the ends of the knotted rope with a flattened ball of sugarpaste. Secure with a little water. If necessary, pinch both ends of the rope before adding the tassels to ensure that it has not become wider. Paint the ropes and tassels in the same gold as previously used.

11 Place a ball of sugarpaste on the edge of the top-tier drape and arrange the gerberas and the gold foliage. Attach the ribbons to the board – the white ribbon first, then run the gold one through the centre.

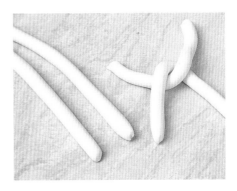

Take two even-sized pieces of rolled sugarpaste and loosely knot them together.

Use boiled water to stick the knots in place and trim to neaten.

Push sugarpaste through a clay gun to form tassels and cut to length.

sugarcraft tips

• In its entirety, this is a very large and expensive cake. In order to achieve the same effect at less cost, you could use a polystyrene dummy for the bottom tier. The remaining three cakes should be more than enough to cater for the average number of wedding guests, which is usually somewhere around 100.

• If you prefer to make both the leaves and the flowers in flowerpaste, mix the metallic dust with some painting solution to produce a wonderfully lustrous effect, when applied to a white base.

• Some sugarpastes will tend to break off when being draped down a cake. In order to make the sugarpaste more 'elastic', mix together equal quantities of sugarpaste and flowerpaste or, alternatively, gelatine paste.

piping

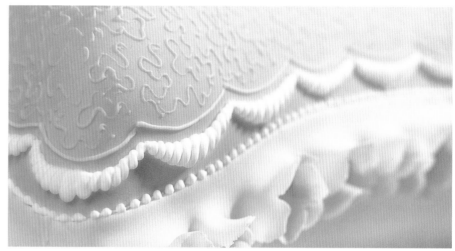

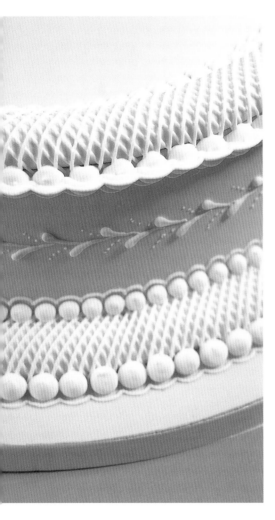

all about piping

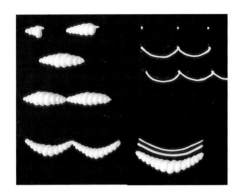

The rope build-up (left) makes a nice accompaniment to fine scallops (right).

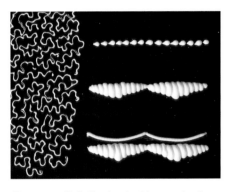

Fine cornelli (left) piped with a no.1 tube. Rope, scallop and snail's trail (right).

Neat pearls piped with a no.2 tube, and 'S' and 'C' scrolls overpiped with a no.1.

Piping is very much a manual skill and requires a great deal of practice to master. Good control is required, whether you are piping choux paste into an éclair or creating a fine string of pearls from royal icing. Whatever the substance being piped, it must be lump free, regardless of the size of the tube (tip) you are using. Equally important, the mixture must not be too runny if you are to maintain a uniform design.

PIPING ROYAL ICING

Queen Victoria gave the royal-iced cake her seal of approval (hence its regal name) and helped to boost its popularity. The Victorians liked to cover every part of their cakes with piped scrolls, lattice and line work, and their designs are still used today, though a little more sparingly. The majority of the basic tools – tubes, piping bags (cones), turntables, palette knives and scrapers – have also remained largely unchanged since Victorian times.

The recipe and instructions for making royal icing appear in the basic techniques chapter (see page 107). It is important to achieve the correct consistency if you wish to produce perfect results. The newly mixed icing should be firm enough to stand to a peak. Never try to pipe onto a wet surface, since it is almost impossible to lift off a mistake without leaving a mark. In contrast, mistakes can easily be lifted off a dry surface.

A general rule of thumb is that the smaller the tube, the smaller the bag you should use for piping. Always be sure to buy good quality paper for your piping bags, because poor quality paper can be weakened easily by wet icing, which may cause it to break when you are mid-flow. This can be disastrous if you are piping a bright colour over a pale base.

When building up lines of piping one on top of another, do not apply more than three lines at a time, and allow each set of lines at least 20 minutes to dry before continuing. Lines will start to lean over if the ones beneath are not dry.

When colouring large quantities of royal icing, it is best to use paste food colourings since liquid ones will soften the consistency and upset the balance of sugar to egg white. To achieve strong colours such as red and black, be sure to read the contents of the colouring matter, because if it contains glycerine the final piece of piped sugar will not set hard. Adding a little powder gum tragacanth will help to alleviate this, but you will have to work very quickly because the icing will start to set in the bag while piping.

PIPING CHOCOLATE

Chocolate cakes have become immensely popular in recent years as people seek alternatives to the traditional fruit wedding cake and, as a result, an increasing number of decorators are becoming interested in chocolate decorating techniques. Chocolate sugarpaste (rolled fondant) is a good starting point, and can be combined with some fairly simple chocolate piping and enhanced with chocolate marzipan roses. Another way of decorating with chocolate that you may like to try is making chocolate cigars/curls by spreading melted chocolate onto a marble slab, leaving it to harden a little and then shaving off curls with a sharp, thin-bladed knife. The curls can then be stuck around the sides of the cake with chocolate buttercream.

You will find that there is a confusing number of different quality chocolates on the market, and not all do the same job. The finest type of chocolate is *couverture* or covering chocolate, which contains a very high proportion of cocoa butter. It needs to be tempered before use – a complicated process that stabilizes the cocoa butter – and is really the province of professional or very experienced cake decorators. As a general rule, any chocolate that contains between 50 and 80 per cent cocoa butter or fat will taste good and do most of the jobs that the average cake decorator requires. Most cake decorating suppliers sell products that can be used without tempering but, if in doubt, check before purchase.

The two main enemies of chocolate are heat and water or steam. Chocolate melts at a very low temperature – the maximum heat before spoiling is just 49°C (120°F) – and water and steam thicken it. Always melt chocolate very gently, either at a low setting in a microwave or in a bowl over a pan of hot water; you will have more control over the temperature of the chocolate with the latter technique. Break the chocolate into small pieces first, particularly when using a microwave, as you can never be sure how much heat will get to the centre and cause spoilage.

White and milk chocolate are more difficult to handle than dark chocolate because they melt at slightly lower temperatures. If heated too high, they thicken very quickly. White chocolate can be coloured

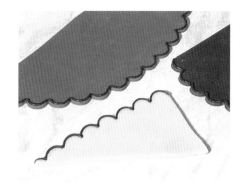

Pipe chocolate around the edges to enhance the scallops.

Pipe embroidery designs, brush icing, cornelli and line flowers on the patches.

Pipe some small scrolls around the base of a cake for a neat finished look.

This delicate piping work is done using slightly thickened chocolate.

Pipe the patterns freehand if you feel confident about your freehand skills.

with glycerine-based paste food colourings and used in conjunction with both dark and milk chocolate. It is especially useful when moulding figures and animals.

Once melted and thickened, chocolate must be left standing in its container in hot water, because it sets quickly and cannot be re-melted to its liquid state. When the chocolate starts to harden at the piping end of the bag, make sure you do not press too hard on the bag to force the chocolate through, as this will only cause the bag to split. Have a plentiful supply of ready-made piping bags to hand. If the chocolate is to be piped directly from the piping bag without a tube, add tiny amounts of water or stock syrup in order to control it. If you have any leftover melted chocolate, wrap it well and save it to grate over a trifle or some ice cream.

Chocolate can be piped through larger tubes to produce shells, using a no.44 star tube (PME), and will leave lines in the shell if the chocolate has been thickened slightly. (The chocolate wedding cake, shown on page 85, offers a fine example of shell piping). Small decorative pieces of chocolate can be piped onto greaseproof (parchment) paper and lifted off when dry. Alternatively, spread the chocolate onto a piece of greaseproof paper, smooth with a palette knife and when quite dry but not set solid, cut out shapes either with a knife or a variety of small cutters, such as circles, squares, diamonds, crescents, etc.

PIPING BUTTERCREAM FLOWERS AND LEAVES

The technique for this particular method of piping is explained in detail in the project instructions of the Buttercream Flowers recipe (see pages 36–40).

The buttercream that is used for piping is made with white fat in order to get the best results, although some people find this most unpalatable. However, there is no doubt that, when buttercream is piped and arranged beautifully on a cake, the overall effect is extremely pleasing. In addition, once the technique has been mastered, it is incredibly fast to execute. So, although many people may not wish to have buttercream flowers as a decoration on a wedding cake, they could certainly be appropriate for smaller, less expensive cakes that need to be produced quickly. This buttercream refrigerates well.

Pipe the leaves in two halves – up one side then down the other.

buttercream for piping

INGREDIENTS

Makes 1.5kg (3lb)

- 1kg (2lb) icing (powdered) sugar
- 120ml (4floz) water
- 500g (1lb) fine, soft, white vegetable shortening
- Pinch of salt
- Food colourings, either paste food colourings or folk art paints

Combine two- and three-dimensional flower designs for best effect.

1 In an electric mixing bowl, combine together the icing (powdered) sugar, water and half the vegetable shortening. Mix gently at first, then beat at a higher speed until you reach a creamy texture. Scrape down any mixture from the sides of the bowl, then beat again until all the ingredients are well blended.

2 Add the remaining amount of shortening, the salt as well as your choice of food colourings then beat for another 5 minutes at a fairly brisk speed. Make sure the bowl is kept covered at all times.

3 Buttercream must be firm for piping both leaves and flowers, so it might be necessary to either add or subtract a little of the water, depending on the weather conditions.

Pipe flowers in a variety of colours and sizes to create a stunning arrangement.

buttercream flowers

I first learned to pipe buttercream flowers in the United States as the Americans are the experts in this field. The secret of success is to keep the buttercream firm, dry and quite crisp. Once you have mastered the skill of piping the leaves and flowers, you will find it is a surprisingly quick method of decorating a cake.

CAKE AND DECORATION

- 13 x 18cm (5 x 7in) and 18 x 23cm (7 x 9in) oval fruit cakes
- 2.5kg (5lb) marzipan
- 3kg (6lb) sugarpaste (rolled fondant)
- 33 x 38cm (13 x 15in) oval cake board
- 500g (1lb) piping buttercream (see page 35)
- Christmas green, spruce (Spectral) and violet (W) paste food colourings
- 250g (8oz) royal icing
- Pink folk art paint (SK)
- 1.5m (2yd) x 1cm (1/2in) pale pink ribbon

ESSENTIAL EQUIPMENT

- Greaseproof (parchment) paper
- 4 small bowls
- Large and small greaseproof paper piping bags (cones)
- No.2 (PME) and either nos.81 and 104 (W) or nos.58 and ST55 (PME) piping tubes (tips)
- Small, thin-bladed palette knife
- Large celstick (or pointed plastic dowel)
- Long-bladed scissors
- Embossed plastic wrap (optional)

1 Cut the smaller of the two cakes in half diagonally, then marzipan both cakes (see page 115). On the top tier, tuck the marzipan about 2.5cm (1in) under the cut edge, then smooth it flat with either your thumbs or a small rolling pin.

2 Cut a piece of greaseproof (parchment) paper the same size as

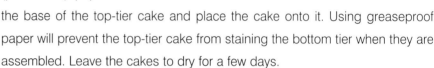

the base of the top-tier cake and place the cake onto it. Using greaseproof paper will prevent the top-tier cake from staining the bottom tier when they are assembled. Leave the cakes to dry for a few days.

3 Once the cakes are dry, cover them with sugarpaste (rolled fondant). Allow both cakes to dry thoroughly before assembling them – one cake on top of the other – onto the cake board.

4 Divide the buttercream into three bowls. (You may require additional bowls, depending on how many different-coloured flowers you wish to use). Colour the buttercream with your choice of paste food colourings and cover until needed.

5 Colour the royal icing pale pink and put it into a piping bag (cone), already fitted with a no.2 tube (tip). Pipe either pearls or small shells around the base of both cakes.

The back of the top tier is also covered with marzipan and sugarpaste.

Position the top tier of the cake at an angle to the bottom tier.

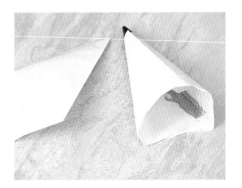

Put pink buttercream along the crease of the bag, then fill with the main leaf colour.

If you find it difficult to pipe good leaf shapes, practise on a cake board first.

Pipe the leaves directly onto the surface of the cake.

6 To pipe the leaves, take one of the large piping bags and fold a deep crease from top to bottom, at the opposite side to where the ends of the bag were originally folded by the manufacturer. Cut off the end and fit in tube no.104 or 58, making sure that the thin edge of the tube is in line with the crease. Using a small, thin-bladed palette knife, stroke some pink buttercream up the creased line, then fill the piping bag with green buttercream. Pipe one side of the leaf first, twisting the tip of the tube over at the top in order to create a point before piping down the other side of the leaf.

7 Establish the position of the large, double-coloured leaves with discreet marks from a scriber or some royal icing. Pipe the leaves as described in step 6. Some colour combinations for the large leaves are cream and green, two shades of green, green and brown, green and yellow, green and red, red and yellow, red and brown, yellow and brown, green and purple.

8 To pipe the flowers, fit a piping bag with tube no.81 or ST55 and fill it with coloured buttercream. Wrap a curl of the buttercream around the tip of the celstick. Then, pipe the petals side by side by pulling the bag upwards from the stick. Initially, the base of the petals will touch the celstick. As each petal is added, turn the stick slightly without turning your hand. Ensure that the petals are close together. Keep adding rows of petals until you reach the required size.

9 Slip the long-bladed scissors around the stick just under the base of the petals, twist the stick and pull downwards, leaving the flower sitting on the scissors. Carefully lift the scissors and take the flower to the surface of the cake. Close the scissors and pull away. Alternatively, use a thin-bladed palette knife in conjunction with the scissors if the buttercream is very soft. When placing the flowers onto the cake, ensure the surface of the cake is flat or, if not, tip the cake up just long enough to allow you to position the flowers. Pipe the flowers in a variety of colours and sizes, to provide more interest to the arrangement.

10 Add extra leaves by putting some green buttercream into a piping bag with no tube. Flatten the end of the bag between finger and thumb, and cut it into an inverted 'V' shape (see page 118). Pipe the leaves by holding the bag flat on the surface of the cake and squeezing until you reach the right size. Pull upwards, breaking off to form a point. To pipe longer leaves, hold the piping bag on its side, flat on the cake surface, squeezing the length of buttercream in a slight curve.

Mark out the position of each leaf and then pipe onto the sugarpaste surface.

Pipe rows of petals around the tip of a celstick until you reach the required size.

Place the blades of a pair of scissors around the base of the flower.

11 Fill some small piping bags (no tubes necessary) with green and another colour buttercream. Cut small holes at the end of the bags, and pipe thin, green stems onto the cake. Dot with the other colour buttercream to make the hollyhocks.

12 For the side drape, first measure around the cake. Colour some of the sugarpaste pink using the folk art paint and roll out the paste into a long strip. If you decide to use an embossed plastic wrap, lay it concave-side-down, press hard then roll over the sugarpaste strip with a rolling pin. Remove the strip and trim the paste to a 5cm (2in) width, saving the trimmings to wrap around the pink drape at measured intervals.

13 Measure the strip of sugarpaste into ten equal sections, marking them with either a small amount of royal icing or a very discreet knife indentation. Then, at each marked section, squeeze the paste together

Twist the celstick and pull downwards to leave the flower sitting on the scissors.

Use a thin-bladed palette knife to slip the flower from the scissors onto the cake.

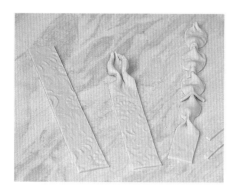

Pinch a strip of sugarpaste at regular intervals and wrap it around the cake.

and wrap the small strips around these narrow sections. Pipe a thick line of royal icing around the side of the bottom-tier cake, lift the centre of the drape and press it gently into place. For both convenience and precision purposes, work on one half of the cake at a time. The join at the back of the cake will not show as it is covered with the small, tucked-over strip.

14 The drape is quite heavy and, to help keep it in place while the royal icing is setting, insert a cocktail stick (toothpick) at an angle under the narrowest sections of the drape. Leave the cocktail stick in position for at least a day, then remove it, making sure that the drape is carefully put back into place.

15 Cover the cake board with your choice of ribbon. For this creation, a pale pink ribbon was preferred.

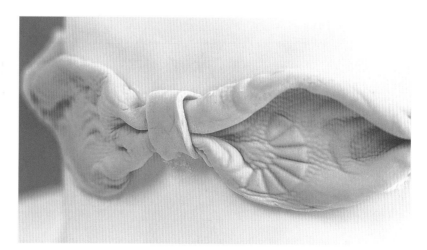

sugarcraft tips

• You can also make the leaves and flowers using royal icing. However, with this method, you would have to make the flowers on greaseproof paper, piping them onto a rose nail, and allow them to dry before attaching them to the cake. You can also pipe the leaves directly onto the cake surface as with buttercream.

• You can use any of the embossed rolling pins now widely available to texture the drape around the centre of the cake.

• The underside of the cake can be marzipanned and sugarpasted instead of using greaseproof paper, but make sure the cake has set hard enough so you can pick it up without leaving finger marks.

victorian splendour

During the research for this cake, I discovered that the Victorians frequently stacked their cakes, which just goes to show that nothing is new! Silk flowers were in vogue at that time – usually arranged in very elaborate alabaster-type vases adorned with cherubs. The beaded strings used in this creation were also popular in Victorian cakes.

CAKE AND DECORATION

- 30cm (12in), 25cm (10in), 20cm (8in) and 15cm (6in) round, rich fruit cakes
- 5kg (10lb) marzipan
- 3.5kg (7lb) icing (powdered) sugar
- 0.5 litre (1 pint/2¹/₂ cups) egg whites
- 41cm (16in), 30cm (12in) round cake boards
- 20cm (8in) and 15cm (6in) thin, round boards
- Metallic silver dusting powder (petal dust) (SK)
- Painting solution (EA)
- 2m (2¹/₄yd) x 1cm (¹/₂in) silver ribbon
- Silver vase
- White delphinium, daisy, pale green and fern flower sprays

ESSENTIAL EQUIPMENT

- Long-bladed knife
- Nos.44 (star) and 4, 3, 2, 1 (plain) piping tubes (tips) (PME)
- Greaseproof (parchment) paper piping bags (cones) in a variety of sizes
- No.4 paintbrush
- Five 15cm (6in) silver cake pillars

1 Marzipan all four cakes following the royal icing technique (see page 105). Allow to dry for a minimum of 4 days – longer if the cakes are being stored in humid conditions.

2 Prepare the royal icing in several batches. Because the icing will not be coloured, there will not be any matching issues. It is much preferable to use fresh batches every 2 to 3 days than to make the required quantity all at once and have to beat it daily and allow it to turn into a weaker consistency.

3 Start by coating the sides of the cake. Allow them to dry before proceeding to the top of the cake. Ice the top with a long-bladed knife, cleaning off the top edge to keep it sharp. Royal-ice cakes are not usually dowelled. One way to ensure that the cakes do not sink is to add a touch of either lemon juice, acetic acid or white vinegar to the icing to harden it and then give the top of the bottom tier at least four coats of this icing. Another option to prevent the cakes from sinking is to ice a firm, thin cake board that will both comfortably fit onto the bottom tier without spoiling the design and hold the pillars that keep the upper tiers stable.

Practise the different shapes you will need to pipe onto the cake.

Pipe 'C' scrolls around the top of the upper tier and at the base of the lower tier.

Build up the depth of the scrolls by piping scroll upon scroll using different tubes.

Starting with a star tube, overpipe twice with a no.4 tube, then use nos.3, 2 and 1.

Pipe a rope outline under the scrolls at the top edges of the cakes.

4 Ice all four cakes separately and on separate boards. Once dry, transfer both the bottom tier and the 25cm (10in) cake onto the thick cake boards, and then ice the boards. Place the two smaller cakes on the thin boards and stack them onto each other, in readiness for piping.

5 Slightly stiffen the royal icing with some icing sugar for piping. For the first scroll, use a star tube (tip) no.44. Pipe a series of freehand 'C' scrolls on the top edge of all the cakes and around the bases of the 30cm (12in) and 25cm (10in) cakes. The remaining two cakes will have pearls piped around the base.

6 To build up the scrolls, first pipe a thick 'C' over the first scroll using a no.4 tube, overpipe with the same tube, switch to tube no.3, then no.2 and finally to no.1. These scrolls do not necessarily have to be done on the same day, particularly the last two lines. It is rather intense work, which can easily strain the eyes.

7 With a no.2 tube, pipe a rope on the side of the cake, under the 'C'-scrolled top edges only. Then, using the same tube, outline all the top and bottom scrolls. Switch to a no.1 tube, then outline and overpipe these same lines.

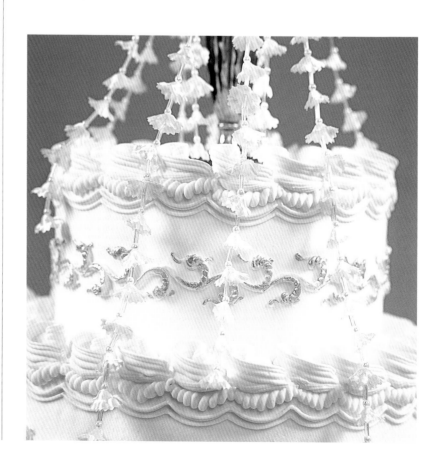

Pipe a plain outline around all the top and bottom scrolls.

Pipe half-plain, half-roped scrolls around the sides of the cakes.

Highlight the scrolls using silver dusting powder mixed with painting solution.

8 Pipe the designs on the sides of the cake freehand. Indicate the centre of the cake with either a discreet indentation from a scriber or a pin, or a little icing. Continue piping the series of 'C' scrolls. Once the piping is done, allow to dry thoroughly. Then, paint the piping with edible metallic silver dusting powder moistened with painting solution.

9 Attach the ribbon around the cake boards, and arrange the flowers in the silver vase. Finally, assemble the cake using the pillars.

sugarcraft tips

• For a pure, sparkling white cake, add a few drops of blue colouring to the royal icing. Make sure to check the blue first with a trial run, as some blues tend to have a greenish tinge.

• Fresh flowers with maiden-hair fern were popular in Victorian times. However, if using fresh flowers, ensure that the vase does not leak.

• The biggest enemy of royal icing is water, so always be extra vigilant not to get any splashes onto the cakes. Marks on royal icing are not easily disguised as water eats into the icing.

• If four tiers prove to be too expensive, use a polystyrene dummy for the bottom tier.

white and mint green trellis

This particular design won me a medal at Hotel Olympia, and I have had a fondness for it ever since. The pale green base colour combined with white provides a certain freshness, accentuated by the lily-of-the-valley and spring flowers. This is not a cake for an inexperienced piper as the trellis work requires absolute precision.

CAKE AND DECORATION

- 25cm (10in) and 15cm (6in) round fruit cakes
- 2kg (4lb) marzipan
- 3kg (6lb) royal icing
- Mint green paste food colouring (Spectral)
- 36cm (14in) and 20cm (8in) round cake boards
- 1.5m (2yd) x 1cm (1/2in) white ribbon
- White and green flowers and leaves (silk, sugar or fresh)
- Small board or shallow florist's white plastic dish

ESSENTIAL EQUIPMENT

- Long-bladed knife
- 2 large plastic piping bags (cones)
- 1cm (1/2in) and 2cm (3/4in) plain piping nozzles (tips)
- Small-bladed knife
- Nos.1 and 3 piping tubes (tips)
- Greaseproof (parchment) paper piping bags (cones)

1 Marzipan the cakes as for royal icing (see page 105). Allow at least 5 days for the marzipan to dry, then place the cakes on their respective boards.

2 Colour about two-thirds of the royal icing pale mint green, reserving the remaining white in a clean bowl. The mint green paste food colouring is quite strong so add it to the icing gradually, using the point of a cocktail stick (toothpick). Keep in mind that, with colour, you can always add, but you cannot take away. To keep the sharp angle on the top edge of the cake, ice the sides of the cake first, then clean off any surplus icing, allow to dry and ice the top. Apply a minimum of two coats, three if possible, making the final coat very thin. Once the cakes are dry, ice both cake boards.

3 Put some white royal icing into the plastic piping bags (cones), each fitted with a different-sized nozzle (tip) – use the smaller nozzle for the top tier. Pipe a thick tube of icing around the top, outside edge of each cake, by holding the bag in one hand and turning the turntable with the other. Where the ends meet, cut the icing with a small-bladed knife, allowing it to slot into place. Smooth the two ends with the knife. Repeat the process on the bottom edge of each cake.

Pipe a thick tube of royal icing around the top edge of each cake.

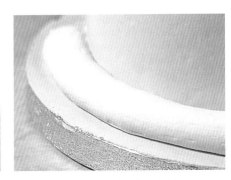

Pipe an identical thick tube of icing around the base of each cake.

45

Pipe fine lines of trelliswork over all four lines of thick icing.

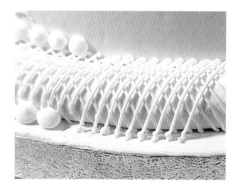

Pipe pearls of icing around the top and bottom of all lines of trelliswork.

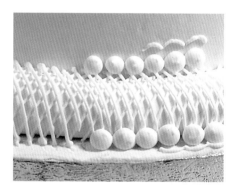

Outline the pearls with small, curved scallops above and below each pearl.

Because the nozzles are large, the tube of icing will be filled with holes. This is nothing to worry about. Leave the thick tube to dry thoroughly, then fill in the holes with some soft icing, blending into a main shape with the small-bladed knife. Sand off any sharp edges with the knife once the icing is completely dry.

4 For the trellis piping, fit a greaseproof (parchment) paper piping bag with a no.1 piping tube (tip). Start piping at a 45 degree angle, first from right to left, then the other way around. Once the trellis work is completed, any roughness in the thick tube of icing will have been completely covered up.

5 Pipe some pearls on each side of the trellis tube using a no.3 tube. When piping them, give the piping bag a half-circle twist of the wrist before pulling off to prevent an unwanted point. Outline the pearls with scallop piping using a no.1 tube, leaving out the pearls located on the top, outside edge of the trellis tube. Pipe the latter on the centre of the pearl and built up with a minimum of three lines of overpiping to achieve the finished effect. Using the no.1 tube, pipe some freehand embroidery around the centre side of the cake.

6 Cover the board with the ribbon, and arrange the flowers and leaves. A posy pick would splinter the surface of the cake, so fix the flowers to either a small board iced the same colour as the cake, or a shallow florist's white plastic dish. Both can be lifted when cutting the cake.

sugarcraft tips

• Coloured royal icing always turns darker when dry. Check the final colour by spreading a little icing onto a spare cake board and allowing it to dry.

• If using royal icing over a number of days, use dried albumen rather than fresh egg white as the icing re-beats and holds its shape better. When colouring royal icing, the chances of reproducing exactly the same colour twice are remote unless you weigh everything to the last gram and add the colour with a dropper.

• When coating the sides and top of the cake, always ensure that the tools you are using – a scraper for the sides and a long-bladed knife for the top – are perfectly straight in order to achieve smooth surfaces.

chocolate patchwork

Patchwork cakes have been around for a long time, but it was something of a challenge to see if it would work using chocolate marzipan. The piping on this cake is all freehand. However, I also offer alternatives for those who feel less confident about their freehand technique.

CAKE AND DECORATION

• 38cm (15in) x 33cm (13in) oval cake board
• 30cm (12in) x 25cm (10in) oval, rich chocolate mud cake (see page 113)
• 1.5kg (3lb) marzipan
• 1kg (2lb) each of white and chocolate sugarpastes (rolled fondant)
• 500g (1lb) white chocolate marzipan (SK) (see page 89)
• 500g (1lb) dark chocolate marzipan (SK) (see page 89)
• 250g (8oz) dark chocolate buttons
• 1.2m (4ft) x 1cm (1/2in) brown ribbon

ESSENTIAL EQUIPMENT

• 46cm (18in) square sheet of greaseproof (parchment) paper
• Long ruler
• Quilting tool
• Small scallop cutter (AB)
• Design wheel (PME)
• Greaseproof (parchment) paper piping bags (cones)

1 Place the oval cake board onto the sheet of greaseproof (parchment) paper. Draw around the oval and cut out the shape. Using a ruler, draw 12 odd shapes onto the cut-out.

2 Marzipan the cake, leave it to dry thoroughly then place it onto its board.

3 Mix together the white and chocolate sugarpastes (rolled fondant). Cover the cake and board with the resulting paste.

4 Lay the pattern on top of the cake, making sure it is absolutely central. With the pointed end of the quilting tool, gently scribe the shapes drawn on the paper. Number each of the shapes from 1 to 12, then cut them out.

5 Roll a small amount each of the white and dark chocolate marzipans into a long tube. Starting in the middle, fold one piece over the other to form a rope, then repeat with the other side. When completed, give a final roll in order to tighten the rope. Lift the rope onto the cake board, tucking it into the base of the cake. At the point where the rope joins, neaten with sloping slices so that the join does not show.

6 Gather the cut pieces of pattern into the main oval shape and work out the colour pattern before rolling out.

Draw a pattern on greaseproof paper and number each piece of the patchwork.

Scribe the pattern onto the soft sugarpaste with a quilting tool.

Make a dark and white chocolate rope to wrap around the base of the cake.

Mix dark and white chocolate marzipan to produce milk chocolate marzipan.

Roll out the marzipans and cut out the required shapes for your patchwork.

7 Roll out and cut the white and dark chocolate pieces first, then mix together the remaining paste to produce the milk colour. Starting with the centre pieces, re-assemble the pieces on a clean, flat surface and, with a small cutter, cut scallops on the outside edge pieces.

8 Following the indented pattern on the top of the cake, place the other pieces into position. The chocolate marzipan is very pliable, making it easy to manipulate into position without spoiling. When all the pieces are in place, use the quilting tool and one of the fancy heads on the design wheel to 'stitch' the pieces around the edges.

9 Put the chocolate buttons into a bowl and stand over hot water until melted. To have more control over the piping chocolate, add a little water to thicken it to a royal icing consistency. Always keep the chocolate standing over hot water, as it will harden more quickly once water has been added to it.

10 Using small piping bags (no tubes necessary), pipe some freehand embroidery, chocolate brush icing, cornelli and line flowers on each of the patches (see page 116). Pipe around the scalloped edges, then pipe a scalloped line around the edge of the cake board. Try to work

Use dark, milk and white chocolate to create a patchwork effect.

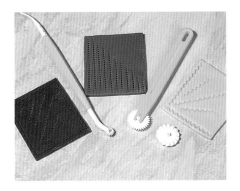

Use a quilting tool with an embroidery wheel attached to simulate stitches.

Pipe the embroidery designs once the patches are in situ.

quickly as the chocolate will set fast, particularly if it is of a high quality. When the chocolate starts to harden at the piping end of the bag, make sure not to press hard on the bag to force the chocolate through as this will only cause the bag to split.

11 If you do not feel confident about your freehand skills, pipe on greaseproof paper over a pattern, lift it off when dry and attach to the patches with a little chocolate to obtain an appliqué-type appearance. Instead of piping, an alternative method is to try rolling out any leftover chocolate marzipan very thinly, and then cutting out some small flowers, leaves and geometric shapes with small blossom cutters, attaching these shapes to the patches to give the impression again of an appliqué appearance.

12 Attach the ribbon to the cake board.

sugarcraft tips

• You will have more control over the temperature of the chocolate if you melt it over hot water rather than in a microwave.

• When piping, you can replace the dark chocolate with white chocolate or even chocolate-coloured royal icing.

pretty cushion

This delicate peach cushion suits a genoese sponge rather than a fruit cake. Carving will be easier if the sponge is at least one day old. The fine cornelli work will provide more texture to the cushion, and you can choose to write a message on the cushion if you wish. Alternatively, arrange some matching flowers.

CAKE AND DECORATION

- 30cm (12in) square genoese sponge (see page 114)
- 500g (1lb) buttercream (see page 35)
- 250g (8oz) jam
- 1kg (2lb) marzipan
- 1kg (2lb) white sugarpaste (rolled fondant)
- 1kg (2lb) peach sugarpaste
- 41cm (16in) square cake board
- 25cm (10in) square, thin board
- 60cm (2ft) cream satin (or any other suitable material)
- Pink paste food colouring (Spectral)
- 250g (8oz) royal icing
- 3 peach silk or sugar roses and leaves

ESSENTIAL EQUIPMENT

- Sharp knife
- Garrett frill cutter
- Bulbous cone tool (PME)
- Greaseproof (parchment) paper piping bags (cones)
- Nos.1 and 2 piping tubes (tips) (PME)

1 Slice the sponge in half and spread with buttercream and jam. Replace the top half, press lightly and clean off any jam or cream that might ooze out.

2 Using a sharp knife, start to carve the sponge into a cushion shape, making a curved cut from one corner to the other and cutting on an angle in towards the centre of the cake. When all four sides have been completed, turn the cake upside down and repeat the process with the underside. Ensure that the sides are not straight, but bulge out to resemble a real cushion.

3 Build up a dome shape using some of the leftover, cut-off pieces of sponge cake. Cover the entire exposed sponge with a light coating of buttercream, then place the cake in the refrigerator.

4 Roll out the marzipan very thinly. Note that in this particular recipe, the marzipan is used to hold the sponge together and provide some firmness to the cushion, rather than as a part of the integral flavour of the cake. Make sure

Cover the sponge cake with a thin layer of marzipan to help keep its shape.

Tuck the marzipan under the cake so that it sticks in place.

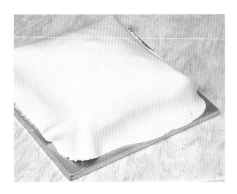

Cover the cake with pale peach sugarpaste and tuck under the edges.

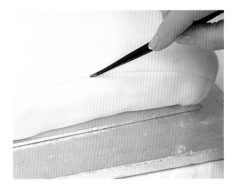

Inscribe a curve along each edge of the cake where the frills will be attached.

Lift the frill at regular intervals to give the impression of movement.

to roll enough marzipan to cover the whole sponge and tuck some underneath. Remove the chilled sponge from the refrigerator and coat it with the marzipan immediately.

5 Save approximately 90g (3oz) of the peach sugarpaste and mix the remainder with the white sugarpaste. Measure the cushion from corner to corner and make sure you add on an extra allowance, which will be folded under the cake. Roll out the sugarpaste to the required measurements. Brush the cake surface with a little boiled water, lift the sugarpaste with a large rolling pin and cover the cake with it. Tuck the paste all around the cake, then place a clean cake board on the top and flip the cake over. Quickly gather up the spare paste in each corner, squeeze together and trim flat with scissors or a sharp knife. Smooth the rest of the paste, then flip the cake back over to its original position.

6 Staple the cream satin to the larger board. Place the cake on the 25cm (10in) cake board before transferring it onto the covered board. If the dome shape has been lost while the cake was turned upside down, push it back into place while the sugarpaste is still soft. Leave the cake for about an hour to allow it to harden a little.

7 Colour the small, reserved piece of peach sugarpaste with a little pink paste food colouring to deepen the overall colour. Cut out seven Garrett frills and, using the bulbous tool, thin out the edges of the frills. Attach the frills to the side centre of the cushion with some royal icing.

8 Cut out another seven frills, this time from the base-colour sugarpaste, roll out in the same manner and secure them onto the cake about 0.5cm (1/4in) above the first frill. In places, lift up the frills to provide an impression of movement.

9 With a no.1 tube (tip), pipe a very small, neat snail trail around the top of the Garrett frill. Then take a no.2 tube and, using a sideways circular motion, with one hand pressing out the icing and the other hand guiding, pipe out a rope. You will need to apply more pressure on the bag as you get nearer the centre of the rope in order to make it fatter. Finally, give the rope an outline by piping a single-line scallop with a no.1 tube.

10 Use a no.1 tube to pipe cornelli over the entire surface of the cake, not forgetting to pipe under the frill down to the board. An alternative to piping cornelli is to pipe clusters of three tiny dots, either white or of different colours. You can also choose to pipe some small 'S' or 'C' scrolls, closely fastened to one another.

11 Piping with small tubes should not be a strenuous task. If you find yourself pressing so hard on the bag that your thumb begins to ache, then your icing is too stiff. Fine piping is a precise art, so ensure that you have enough light to work with, especially when overpiping or piping white on white.

12 Arrange both the roses and leaves on top of the cake, then fasten them with either a little royal icing or a very small amount of the coloured sugarpaste.

The lower frill is a slightly deeper shade than the upper frill.

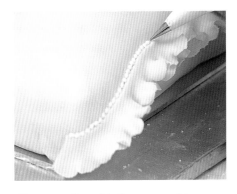

Pipe a small snail trail or a row of tiny pearls above the top of the frills.

Pipe a rope and scallops above the frill, then cover the cake with piped cornelli.

sugarcraft tips

• It is not considered hygienic for a cake to come into contact with fabric. Therefore, in cases where the cake is being presented on such a surface, ensure that the cake is resting on a cake board, to act as a barrier between the cake and the fabric.

• You could replace the genoese sponge with a rich fruit cake. However, with the fruit cake, there will be quite a lot of wastage when carving the shape. Use the extra pieces of cake to make truffles or miniature puddings.

• A day-old genoese sponge will be much easier to carve than a very fresh one. Do not keep a sponge cake for more than a week.

painting

all about painting

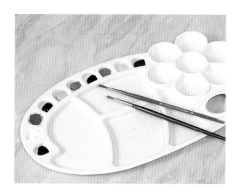

Instead of a large plate or tile, use a palette with dimples for holding paints.

Some basic brush strokes can be used for leaves or petals.

Build up brush strokes for a simple rose. Load the brush with white and a colour.

Painting techniques produce some of the most beautiful and impressive decorated cakes. Many people are wary of trying painting techniques because they cannot draw, but in fact you can trace designs if you do not feel confident painting freehand. There are many good books available containing folk art or similar designs that you can use as inspiration. The key to success is to practise the design first before painting it onto the cake.

PAINTING WITH FOLK ART PAINTS

Folk art paints are edible, two of the main ingredients being starch and glucose. They can be applied to sugarpaste (rolled fondant), royal icing, marzipan, flowerpaste, gelatine paste, pastillage and porcelain paste without bleeding. They can also be added to buttercream to produce bright, vivid colours (the starch in the paint binds with the fat in the buttercream, unlike water-based colours). You can also add folk art paints to royal icing to produce pastel colours, but they are not recommended for creating strong colours since too much paint will cause the icing to break down.

equipment

• Good quality paintbrushes ranging from a no.4 to a 00 if you intend to paint very fine detail

• Fairly thick, old paintbrushes to mix the paints

• Large plate or flat tile

• Small palette knife

• Couple of cups or small bowls for water

• Plenty of tea (kitchen) towels

• Patterns, sketches and pictures, either to copy freehand or to trace onto the cake or plaque

Use a scribing tool to imprint the design from a tracing paper pattern onto the cake, or trace it using a non-graphite pencil. Alternatively, pipe the design onto a sheet of glass and carefully press the piped design onto the surface of the cake (please note that this method is suitable for sugarpaste only).

With a palette knife, take a little paint from its container and put it onto either a tile or plate. Effects as diverse as oil painting to washes can be achieved. The thicker the paint, the more like oils it will be. If you need to thin the paint in order to produce a wash, add a little water and mix it in with an old paintbrush. For folk art painting, it is important that the brush is fully loaded with paint, particularly for leaves and flowers. More than one colour at a time can be loaded onto the brush to produce effects of light and shade, or you can mix several colours on the plate. The range of hues available in folk art paints is quite comprehensive. By mixing colours, almost any combination in the spectrum is possible.

Lay the whole of the loaded brush onto the surface of the cake or plaque, either starting at the tip and lowering all the brush onto the cake as you pull it down, or laying the whole brush on the cake and gradually lifting it up to the tip before pulling it off the surface. Your aim should be to use simple, fluid strokes that can ultimately be turned into leaves, flowers and scrolls.

If you lay one wet colour next to another wet colour, they will not run into each other but will blend together. Folk art paints dry in around 20 minutes, but can become a little sticky if the weather is very humid. If you agitate the brushes too vigorously you are liable to wear out the bristles. If you are new to painting with folk art paints, it is a good idea to practise on a piece of scrap paper before you try it for real. For additional advice and tips on folk art painting, a video called *Something Colourful* is available from Videopoint (see Suppliers).

PAINTING WITH METALLICS

The advent of edible metallics has caused a great deal of excitement among cake decorators. It has now become both easy and fashionable to use gold, silver and a whole range of metallic food colourings to enhance cake decoration. The two main methods of application are painting and dusting. When painting, mix the colour with painting solution (an edible alcohol- and citrus oil-based solution). Then, apply the paint onto the surface of the cake or, alternatively, pick out features of an embossed design of your choice.

The next stage is to embellish the basic leaf shapes in a folk art style.

The finished rose is highlighted with tiny dabs of white paint.

You can use a variety of metallic paints to embellish the buttons.

fairies

With such a wide variety of petal dusts, edible metallics and paste food colourings now available, it was a real pleasure to paint and colour these different fairy figures. Fairy cakes are extremely popular but painting the delicate faces is a true challenge.

CAKE AND DECORATION

- 25cm (10in) round, rich fruit cake
- 1.5kg (3lb) marzipan
- 2kg (4lb) sugarpaste (rolled fondant)
- Egg yellow and caramel paste food colourings (Spectral)
- 36cm (14in) round cake board
- Plasticine
- Moulding gel (AB)
- Fairy plaster models
- Sapphire, jade and ruby moonbeam food colourings (SK)
- Lavender, mid-blue, iris, white satin and golden rose dusting powders (petal dusts) (EA)
- Painting solution (EA)
- Pink, peach, champagne and white satin dusting powders (petal dusts)
- Red, olive green, black, brown, yellow, saffron and rose folk art paints (SK)
- 100g (4oz) gelatine paste or flowerpaste (see pages 111–12)
- Cornflour (cornstarch)
- 250g (8oz) royal icing
- 1.3m (1¹/₂yd) x 1cm (¹/₂in) ribbon

ESSENTIAL EQUIPMENT

- Nos.4, 2, 1 and 000 paintbrushes
- Plate or tile
- Large frame cutter (Code H, AP)
- Greaseproof (parchment) paper piping bags (cones)
- Nos.2, 1.5, 1 and 0 piping tubes (tips)

1 Marzipan the cake and leave it to dry for a few days.

2 Colour some of the sugarpaste (rolled fondant) cream, using very small amounts of both the egg yellow and caramel paste food colourings. Place the cake onto its board and cover both with the cream sugarpaste. Leave the rest of the sugarpaste white for the fairies.

3 Make the fairy moulds using the plasticine and moulding gel (see page 109). Press some white sugarpaste into the moulds and trim the excess. Leave for 10 minutes, then un-mould. Set aside until the paste figures are thoroughly dry.

4 To paint the dry fairy figures, match the colouring of the fairies with the type of flower they represent. For this particular cake I have chosen a rose, a daisy, a daffodil, a hydrangea and a delphinium.

5 Start by painting the wings, using the three moonbeam dusting powders (petal dusts) mixed with a little painting solution except for the daisy fairy, whose wings are painted with the white satin dust mixed with some painting solution. Paint the clothes of both the delphinium and hydrangea fairies with the lavender,

Use moulding gel and plaster models to make fairy moulds.

Ease the plaster models out of the set moulding gel, ready to make the fairies.

Gently ease the sugarpaste figure out of the flexible mould.

When the fairies are thoroughly dry, paint them in your chosen colours.

Start by painting the fairies' wings using the moonbeam food colourings.

mid-blue and iris dusting powders mixed with a little painting solution. Paint the other fairies with the folk art paints. To achieve the flesh colour, mix together the peach, champagne and white dusting powders and, very lightly, dust dry onto the fairies' arms, legs and faces.

6 Finally paint the eyes, mouth and eyebrows, using a very fine brush, or, alternatively, pick out the hairs in a thicker brush until you are left with three or four. The models are so tiny that it will be almost impossible to paint open eyes and keep them in proportion. Painting a downward crescent for the eyes will be equally effective. Use a mere whisper of the pink dusting powder to highlight the cheeks.

7 Roll out the gelatine paste or flowerpaste very thinly, and cut out a plaque with the frame cutter. Dust a flat cake board with some cornflour (cornstarch) and, with a palette knife, place the plaque on the board. Leave to dry for 1 day then turn the plaque over.

8 Fit a piping bag (cone) with a no.0 tube (tip) and fill with royal icing. Pipe around the edges of the plaque. Leave to dry, then mix some golden rose dusting powders with a little painting solution and paint over the piped line. Place the plaque in position on top of the cake.

Starting with a no.1.5 tube, outline the edges of the plaque. Switch to a no.1 tube and continue piping and overpiping until the design is three lines deep and three lines wide. Then, ornate the top edge of the cake with a scalloped pattern by first marking the intervals between the scallops with a little royal icing, then piping some scallops freehand, respecting the intervals.

9 Measure around the cake and divide into six equal sections. Mark the sections with a little icing. Attach all the fairies in between those sections to the side of the cake with some royal icing. Remember to attach a fairy to the plaque at the top.

10 Paint the grass and the small hollyhock-type flowers freehand and in a fairly random style on the plaque and around the base of the cake.

11 Fit a piping bag with a no.2 tube and fill with royal icing. Pipe some pearls around the base of the cake and attach a ribbon around the cake board. A ribbon with a flower design would be appropriate for this particular cake.

sugarcraft tips

• The fairy models used in this cake were purchased in a craft shop. You can also use fridge magnets, or venture into toy and art shops.

• When the fairy moulds are no longer needed, cut up the moulding gel and put it back into the pot to be re-melted. In this way, you are not left with a mould that may never be used again.

• Use a magnifying lamp to assist you when painting the faces of the fairies. It will make the job a lot easier.

Pipe around the edges of the plaque with a no.0 tube, then paint gold.

Use a very fine paintbrush to paint grass and flowers on the plaque.

Paint flowers and grass around the base of the cake to match those on the plaque.

floral cake

The build-up of simple brush strokes will ultimately evolve into a delicate floral pattern. Ornate the cake with silk or sugar flowers. Use asters for a lilac, purple and pink cake, daisies if you prefer a yellow, brown and gold combination and dahlias if you are after a red, peach and copper look.

CAKE AND DECORATION

- 25cm (10in) and 20cm (8in) petal-shaped fruit cakes, 9cm (3¹/2in) deep
- 3kg (6lb) marzipan
- 38cm (15in) and 33cm (13in) petal-shaped cake boards
- 3.5kg (7lb) sugarpaste (rolled fondant)
- 20cm (8in) thin, petal-shaped board
- 250g (8oz) royal icing
- Red, yellow, saffron, olive green, black and white folk art paints (SK)
- 7.5cm (3in) thin, round board
- 2 large yellowy orange silk or sugar chrysanthemums
- 2 yellow cosmos and extra buds
- 5 brick red silk or sugar daisies
- 5 pale peach silk or sugar daisies
- 1 pale lemon silk or sugar daisy
- 2.25m (2¹/2yd) x 1cm (¹/2in) white ribbon

ESSENTIAL EQUIPMENT

- Straight Garrett frill cutter
- Celstick
- Greaseproof (parchment) paper piping bags (cones)
- Nos.1 and 2 piping tubes (tips)
- Plate or tile
- Nos.4, 2 and 1 paintbrushes

1 Marzipan the cakes and allow them to dry. Cover both the cakes and the boards with sugarpaste (rolled fondant). Allow them to dry, then slip a thin petal board under the top-tier cake before placing it onto the larger cake.

2 Roll out some paste quite thinly and cut out six straight Garrett frills. Cover the frills with a piece of plastic to prevent them from drying. Taking frills one at a time, turn the cutter around and cut a scalloped edge along the straight-edged side. With a celstick, make a round hole on both sides of each scallop, then cut the frill in half.

3 Fill a piping bag (cone) with royal icing and pipe a line near the base of the petal curve. Since you have cut the Garrett frill in half, you can pipe two frills at a time. Attach a frill to each curve, trimming off any surplus so the joins are in the exact centre of the curving petal shape. Repeat this process on the second cake.

4 Using a no.1 piping tube (tip), pipe around each hole and scallop shape on all the frills. Then, using a no.2 tube, pipe some pearls around the base of both cakes. Leave to dry thoroughly.

Scallop and make holes in the frills, then place them around the base of the cakes.

Pipe royal icing around each hole and scallop, then pipe pearls around the base.

Paint the daisies on the cakes using a series of single brush strokes.

Paint leaves around the flowers and, if necessary, add more daisies for balance.

Try to paint the tendrils of foliage as if they were growing up the side of the cakes.

5 Spread your paints onto a plate or tile, preferably white to give a realistic idea of the colour, which is essential if you are mixing colours. When mixing colours with either water or each other, make sure to use an old paintbrush. The action of vigorously agitating the brush will wear out the bristles. If you are new to this method of decorating, practise on a spare piece of paper before starting on the cake. Scribing on the cake is not recommended, as the paint will fall into the grooves and distort the finished flower.

6 Mark out the position of each of the main flowers with a touch of icing. Then, paint the daisies with a series of single brush strokes of varying thicknesses. Vary the length of the petals to add a different perspective to the flower. Allow the flowers to dry, then paint the leaves around the flowers.

7 Paint some flowers onto the cake board, once the main design has been completed. Add leaves and curlicues as a final touch to lend an overall balance to the cake design.

Place a mound of sugarpaste onto a paste-covered board on top of the cake.

8 Attach a mound of sugarpaste onto the small, covered cake board and place it in the centre of the top-tier cake. Pipe small pearls around the edge of the board. When dry, arrange the flowers.

9 Arrange four daisies onto the cake randomly, securing them with a little royal icing. The flowers will add a third dimension to the cake and reduce the 'flatness' of the painted area.

10 Place the cakes onto the second largest sugarpasted board. Paint a few more flowers, leaves and curlicues onto the board to enhance the continuity of design. Attach the ribbon to the edges of the boards.

Continue the floral design on the edge of the covered cake board.

Add in leaves and curlicues to the flower. One or two flowers will suffice.

sugarcraft tips

• Adding black to a colour will shade it. White will highlight.

• Try making your own sugar flowers with white flowerpaste. Paint them with the same folk art paints as the painted flowers to achieve a more harmonious display.

• Because glucose is one of the ingredients of the edible paints, you will find that the resulting surface is slightly shiny, even when the paint is dry.

folk art cake

Most European countries have their own distinctive style of folk art, providing a vast array of innovative designs for those who wish to explore this specific type of cake-decorating work. For this particular cake, I opted for the combination of leaves and scrolled ornaments as an exciting substitute for flowers.

CAKE AND DECORATION

- 30cm (12in) octagonal, rich fruit cake, 9cm (3¹/₂in) deep
- 3.5kg (7lb) marzipan
- 36cm (14in) octagonal cake board
- 46cm (18in) round cake board
- 7.5cm (3in) thin, round board
- 4kg (8lb) sugarpaste (rolled fondant)
- Black, white, red, blue, yellow, saffron, olive green, pink, heather and brown folk art paints (SK)
- 500g (1lb) royal icing
- Selection of silk or sugar leaves
- 1.5m (5ft) x 1cm (¹/₂in) dark green ribbon

ESSENTIAL EQUIPMENT

- Large palette knife
- Patterns (optional)
- Tracing paper (optional)
- Scriber or non-graphite pencil (optional)
- Nos.6, 4, 3, 2, 1 and 0 good quality, sable paintbrushes
- Old brush
- Large plate or tile
- Greaseproof (parchment) paper piping bags (cones)
- Nos.2 and 1.5 piping tubes (tips)

1 Marzipan the cake and place it on the octagonal cake board. At the same time coat the two round cake boards with sugarpaste (rolled fondant). Leave to dry thoroughly for a couple of days.

2 Sugarpaste the cake and octagonal board at the same time, taking the paste right over the edge of the board. Transfer to either a smaller board or something that will raise it off the surface of the table and allow the sugarpaste around the board to dry. Once dry, slip a large palette knife under the cake and transfer to the larger round board. Remove your hand and draw out the knife.

3 There are a variety of methods for painting the sides. Try painting freehand, either copying the templates (see pages 117–118) or using your own, or draw the patterns onto tracing paper and then scribe them onto the cake. Another option is to trace the patterns directly onto the cake with a non-graphite pencil. If using this method, ensure that the patterns are not facing each other in a mirror effect, by tracing the pattern on both the front and the back of the tracing paper. To keep the pattern firm, secure the tracing paper to the cake with icing, which will also free both your hands for drawing.

Trace the pattern onto the side of the cake using a non-graphite pencil.

Alternatively, place the tracing paper onto the cake and lightly scribe the pattern.

Once the design has been drawn or transferred to the cake, painting can start.

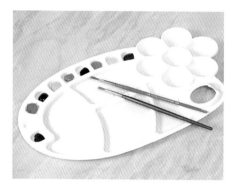

Use fine paintbrushes and a palette to hold the different colours you will need.

Paint the patterns as desired, applying the colours in long, even strokes.

4 Once the designs are in place, slightly tilt the cake as a means to make the painting easier. When painting, try to support one hand with the other, and to rest your elbows at a comfortable angle. Fully load your brushes with paint for most strokes. Use the white folk art paint to highlight the edges of the leaves. Once the painting is completed, allow to dry thoroughly.

5 To erase any mistakes from the surface of the cake, first wipe with a clean, damp, smooth-surfaced cloth. Then, load a thick paintbrush with cornflour (cornstarch) and dab on the area. Brush once more, this time with a clean paintbrush. This technique will work even with red and black paints, but it must be done immediately, before the paint has had a chance to dry.

6 Once all the painting is dry, pipe some pearls or small shells around the base of the cake, using a no.2 piping tube (tip). Then, with a 1.5 tube, pipe a few 'C' scrolls in the left-hand corner of each panel as well as on the largest cake board.

7 Arrange the foliage on the small covered cake board, securing it with a little sugarpaste. The foliage can be either silk or sugar. Then, place the board onto the top of the cake and pipe some small pearls around it in order to mask the edges.

8 Attach the dark green ribbon around the large board.

Load your brush fully with the main colour and a touch of white for highlights.

sugarcraft tips

• Folk art paints are completely edible, and therefore can be quite safely eaten once the cake is cut.

• There are numerous books readily available on folk art painting if you are interested in learning more about the differing styles throughout the world or the various stroke techniques. A good place to start is the local library.

• Classes on folk art painting are also increasingly popular. Any style that can be painted onto wood can equally be painted onto a cake.

Lay your brush on the cake firmly and try to paint the shapes in single, fluid strokes.

You can blend colours by overpainting as well as using two colours simultaneously.

buttons and berries

You can personalize this cake by using a wider variety of buttons than I have used. Try selecting buttons in different sizes and colours. The main coffee colour will marry itself to most metallic colours. If you wish to keep a harmony of round shapes, use berries for the top centrepiece.

CAKE AND DECORATION

- 25cm (10in), 20cm (8in) and 15cm (6in) round fruit cakes, 10cm (4in) deep
- 4.5kg (9lb) marzipan
- 20cm (8in) and 15cm (6in) thin, round boards
- 3.5kg (7lb) sugarpaste (rolled fondant)
- Caramel, dark brown and chestnut paste food colourings
- 36cm (14in) round cake board
- 250g (8oz) royal icing
- Red copper satin, golden rose and bronze satin dusting powders (petal dusts) (EA)
- Assorted plastic, silk or sugar berries
- 1.2m (1¹/₂yd) x 1cm (¹/₂in) chestnut brown ribbon

ESSENTIAL EQUIPMENT

- Assorted buttons
- Moulding gel (AB)
- Measuring tape
- Sheet of greaseproof (parchment) paper
- Stainless steel coloured-head pins
- Greaseproof (parchment) paper piping bags (cones)
- Ruler
- Sharp knife
- No.2 piping tube (tip)
- Posy pick

1 Marzipan the cakes and leave to dry thoroughly for about 4 to 5 days.

2 Make moulds of the buttons with the moulding gel (see page 109).

3 Colour the sugarpaste (rolled fondant) pale coffee using both the caramel and dark brown paste food colourings. Cover the three cakes and board with the resulting coffee paste. Allow to dry for a minimum of 3 days. If desired, you can dowel the bottom and middle tiers (see page 110).

4 Measure around each cake. Then, cut some strips of greaseproof (parchment) paper of the circumference of each cake and about 2.5cm (1in) wide. Fold each strip into half three times, then press the folds very hard with your thumbnail to get a good, sharp crease. When you open the folds out, there will be eight equal sections to the strip.

5 Pin the paper patterns onto each cake, starting at the bottom of the bevelled top edge of the cake. Insert the first row of pins into every other crease, to obtain four equal sections. Then, insert the second row into the remaining four creases, 7.5cm (3in) up from the board. It is from these pinpoints that the loops

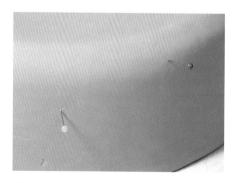

The loops of twisted paste will start flowing from these pinpoints.

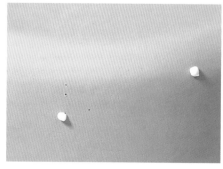

Remove the paper pattern and mark the pin pricks with dots of royal icing.

Twist sugarpaste strips by holding each end and turning in opposite directions.

Attach the twisted sugarpaste strips to the dots of icing.

Choose which button moulds you wish to use on each tier of the cake.

of twisted paste will start. These loops must fall evenly all the way around the cakes and, therefore, you need to mark the lowest point where the loop will fall. Insert a pin at the lowest falling point of the highest loop, about 4cm (1¹/₂in) up from the base of the cake. This mark will also be the starting point for the lowest loop. Also insert a pin to mark the lowest point for the second loop, 2.5cm (1in) up from the base. Once the pins are in place, make a small mark in the paste on either side of the pins, then remove all the pins.

6 Colour the remaining paste a deeper hue by adding more caramel and a touch of chestnut. In order for the royal icing to blend with the coffee colour of the cake, colour it, using the caramel and dark brown paste food colourings. Fill a piping bag (cone) with the coloured icing (no tube necessary). Roll out the paste very thinly and, with a ruler, cut eight strips 23cm (9in) by 1cm (¹/₂in) for the top tier, eight strips 19cm (7¹/₂in) by 1cm (¹/₂in) for the middle tier and eight strips 15cm (6in) by 1cm (¹/₂in) for the top tier. Cover the strips with a sheet of plastic paper to prevent them from drying out.

7 Starting with the four highest points on the bottom tier, pipe a dot of icing on each pin mark, twist a strip of sugarpaste and attach firmly to the icing sugar. Swing it across and attach to the second dot of icing. Continue this process all the way around the cake. As the sugarpaste

strips are rather heavy, they will tend to sag and eventually fall off unless supported. You have already made a mark to indicate the lowest edge of the loop so, once again, insert a pin just under the paste to support the loop. Continue this process around the cake with the second row of loops. Repeat on all three cakes. Finally, stack the cakes, making sure that all the points line up.

8 Using a no.2 tube, pipe some pearls with the coloured royal icing around the bases of all three cakes.

9 Make the sugarpaste buttons by pressing the remaining paste into the moulds. You will need eight buttons per cake. It is best to allow the moulded buttons to harden for at least 2 to 4 days, so they are easier to handle. Dust or paint the buttons with a variety of dusting powders (petal dusts). Then, colour some of the berries with the same dusting powders, mixed with painting solution if desired.

10 Attach the buttons at the joining points of the twisted strips with a small amount of the dark sugarpaste and a little boiled water. Smooth the small amount of sugarpaste outwards and towards the surface of the cake in order to hide the joins. Secure the button in place with a pin, until well stuck.

11 Attach the ribbon around the cake board. Insert a posy pick into the top tier and arrange the berries in it. This cake will make a perfect autumn wedding cake. Select some berries that will best complement the colour scheme of the wedding.

sugarcraft tips

• If the sugarpaste keeps breaking when being twisted and looped across, add a small amount of gelatine paste or flowerpaste to give it more elasticity.

• This cake could easily be transformed into a stunning Christmas cake. Leave the sugarpaste white and colour the buttons silver. Add a top decoration of holly leaves or a combination of berries and mistletoe to provide a true festive aura.

• If preferred, replace the buttons with bows and paint the loops to match. If you decide to paint the loops, make sure to slip a thin sheet of paper between the loop and the cake before proceeding with the painting, so that no paint spills onto the cake.

Remove the sugarpaste from the moulds, then dust or paint with dusting powders.

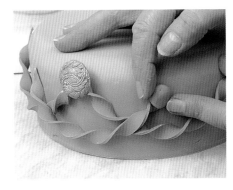

Smooth a small amount of sugarpaste over the joins of each twisted swag.

Dampen the paste with a little boiled water and attach a button.

decorated tile cake

This cake was originally commissioned by *Cakes & Sugarcraft* magazine. They wanted a cake the shape of a cube with all four sides decorated with wall tile designs, using edible paints. The cube is ornamented with tile shards in odd lengths, embedded into the top surface. Use tall shards to balance the cake.

CAKE AND DECORATION

- Two 20cm (8in) square fruit cakes, 9cm (3^1/$_2$in) deep
- 2kg (4lb) marzipan
- Icing (powdered) sugar
- 30cm (12in) and 41cm (16in) square cake boards
- 250g (8oz) sugarpaste (rolled fondant)
- Two 400g (13oz) packets white flowerpaste (SK)
- Cornflour (cornstarch)
- 2kg (4lb) royal icing
- 1.75m (2yd) white ribbon
- Selection of folk art paints (SK)

ESSENTIAL EQUIPMENT

- Long-bladed knife or steel ruler
- 2 smoothers
- Small palette knife
- Plate or tile
- Nos.4 and 1 good quality sable paintbrushes
- Greaseproof (parchment) paper piping bags (cones)
- No.2 piping tube (tip)
- Scriber
- Scalpel

1 Sandwich the two cakes together with marzipan, then marzipan the top of this newly formed cake. Lightly dust the working area with icing (powdered) sugar and place the cake top down onto the dusted area. Cut four squares of marzipan to the exact measurements of the cube and cover all four sides with the individual marzipan squares. The marzipan will keep the cube shape sharp and straight. Then, butt the corners of the cube with two smoothers. Leave the cube to dry overnight, making sure that the cake is not sticking to the table by gently moving it occasionally. The following day, turn the cake the correct way up and place it on the 30cm (12in) board.

2 Mix equal quantities of sugarpaste (rolled fondant) and flowerpaste. Roll out enough paste to make four square tiles to the measurements of the sides of the cube. However, remember that the sides of the cube will be larger once the cake is iced, so allow for slightly larger tiles. While the paste is still soft, mark out some tile shapes with the back of a long-bladed knife or a steel ruler. Then, dust a firm cake board or tray with cornflour (cornstarch), place the tiles on it and leave them for at least 4 days to dry thoroughly. Turn the tiles once a day.

Marzipan and royal ice the cake cube and allow it to dry thoroughly.

Prepare the four tiles and cut one extra to cut into rough shards.

Draw or trace your chosen designs onto the square tiles.

Paint the designs, working from the top to the bottom of each tile.

Attach a painted tile to each side of the cake with royal icing.

3 With the leftover paste, roll out another tile, cut it into shards and leave them to dry. These shards will be assembled on top of the cake.

4 The cake needs to be royal iced in order to maintain a straight cube shape. Ice two opposite sides by evenly spreading some royal icing, using a palette knife. Then, draw up a long-bladed knife or a ruler from the base of the cake to the top edge in one, even stroke. Allow to dry, then repeat the procedure on the two remaining sides. Ice the top of the cake, smoothing royal icing over the surface with a palette knife. Then, once again, draw the long-bladed knife from the far edge of the cake towards you in one, even stroke. Apply a minimum of two coats of royal icing on all the sides.

5 Ice the board once the cake is dry. Royal ice the larger cake board. Add a little water to some royal icing until you achieve a run-out consistency. Pour over the board and smooth with a long-bladed knife. Hit the board sharply against the table to bring up any air bubbles. Allow to dry thoroughly, then place the other board with the cake on top of it. Attach the white ribbon around the edges of the iced board.

6 Select a design to paint on the tiles. Use the templates supplied on pages 120–23, or inspire yourself from art books covering tiles through the ages. Sketch out your chosen design(s) to the correct dimensions on a sheet of drawing paper.

7 Once you are satisfied with the design, select your colour scheme. There are two painting techniques possible. Choose your preferred technique according to your drawing skills. One option is to freehand the design from your original sketch directly onto the tile. You can also

trace your sketch with a non-toxic pencil and transfer the design onto the tile. Make sure not to break the tile by applying too much pressure. You should start painting from the top of the tile and work your way down. Mix your chosen colours on a plate and thin them down with a little

water. If you would like to achieve an oil-like finish, reduce the amount of water considerably. In my creation, one of the tiles uses less colours than the others. Many tiles, particularly the Dutch ones, are painted with country scenes and only use a single colour. The possibilities are endless, so use a colour scheme that best suits the occasion.

8 Spread a little royal icing onto each side of the cake then attach each painted tile to its appropriate side carefully.

9 Pipe some pearls or small shells with a no.2 tube (tip) at the base of the cake, down each corner edge and around the top, inside edge.

10 Paint the shards with parts of the designs, to give the impression of a broken tile. With a scriber or a cocktail stick (toothpick), make a light scratch where you wish to place the shards on the cake. Then, with a scalpel, cut some slits on the top surface of the cake. Widen the slits so the shard can fit in snugly. Pipe a line of royal icing into the slit and ease in the shard, starting with the tallest one. You may have to prop up the shards until the icing has set.

11 If desired, texture either one or both cake boards with dot clusters or very fine cornelli work.

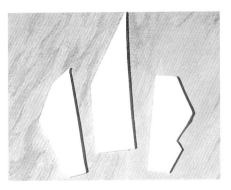

Lay out the sugarpaste shards and decide which patterns to paint on them.

Paint the patterns so that they are cut off at the edges to look like a broken tile.

Pipe a line of royal icing into a slit on the top of the cake and insert the shard.

sugarcraft tips

• If using a sponge cake, use 500g (1lb) less marzipan than the amount needed for the fruit cake, as the layer of marzipan should be slightly thinner or its weight could cause the cake to buckle.

• Cornflour absorbs moisture and can be used to speed up the drying process for the tiles.

• Practise painting on a sheet of paper the same size as your tile.

• Use a white paint to highlight the shape of a petal or a leaf.

broderie anglaise

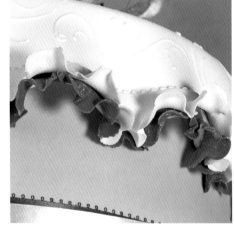

all about broderie anglaise

Roll sugarpaste evenly over the top of a cake that has royal-iced sides.

Smooth the edges of the sugarpaste into the royal icing to produce a slight bevel.

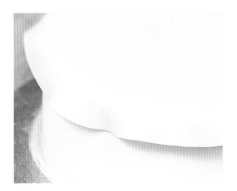

Place a larger circle of thin sugarpaste over the cake to hang like a tablecloth.

Broderie anglaise designs are ideal for decorating cakes and produce extremely pretty cake edgings. One of the most popular cake decorations is to apply royal icing around the sides of the cake and a sugarpaste (rolled fondant) tablecloth over the top with a broderie anglaise edging attached to it. There are many variations on this theme.

BRODERIE ANGLAISE EDGING

Marzipan the cake in the same way as for royal icing (see page 105) and let it dry for 3 to 4 days. Place the cake in the centre of the board on a turntable and royal ice the sides only. Allow to dry completely, then apply another coat of royal icing. Ice the board and let it dry thoroughly.

Roll out a circle of sugarpaste about 5mm (1/4in) thick and cut to the size of the top of the cake. Brush boiled water onto the marzipanned cake surface and lift the disc of sugarpaste with a rolling pin. Position the disc on top of the cake by lightly rolling the pin over the surface. Trim the surplus sugarpaste and press down the edges with a thumb or smoother. Make sure there is no marzipan showing.

Roll out sugarpaste about 3mm (1/8in) thick and cut a circle approximately 3.5cm (11/2in) larger than the top of the cake. Use a paper template for this if you wish. Lift up the circle of sugarpaste with a rolling pin and place it over the top of the cake like a tablecloth. Adjust the paste if necessary so that it overlaps the cake evenly all the way around. Trim with scissors if necessary. Lift up the tablecloth here and there, and dab the underside with a little boiled water to stick it in place. Allow it to firm up for about an hour.

Measure around the edge of the tablecloth and divide this figure by 51/2 (length of the cutter) to ascertain the number of broderie anglaise frills to cut out. It is almost always the case that an exact number of frills is not required and that you will need to insert a section of one frill. If this happens, simply ensure that you position the odd section out of view at the back of the cake, or cover it up with a flower spray.

Roll out some sugarpaste as thinly as possible, cut out the required number of frills using either the cutters or the templates on page 124, and cover with plastic. Cut out eyelet holes or emboss the sugarpaste, keeping it covered at all times.

With a no.1 tube (tip) and royal icing, pipe a thin line around the edge of the tablecloth. Pipe the length of one frill at a time. Attach the frills to the tablecloth, butting them together; do not overlap them. If you are left with an uneven gap between the first and last frill, cut the odd piece from a whole frill and position it at the back of the cake.

Using a straight Garrett frill cutter and very thin paste, cut half the previous number of frills. Turn the cutter around and cut scallops along the straight edge. Slice the frills in half so that each narrow frill has a straight edge and a scalloped edge. Cover the frills with plastic and use a celstick to make a hole above each of the scallops. Pipe a line of royal icing about 5mm (^{1}/4in) above the wide broderie anglaise frill and attach the narrow frills, again making sure that all joins butt together and do not overlap. With a no.1 tube and royal icing, pipe a small snail trail or row of pearls around the top edge of the upper frill where it touches the cake. With a no.0 tube, pipe around all edges of the broderie anglaise, including any holes that have been cut out.

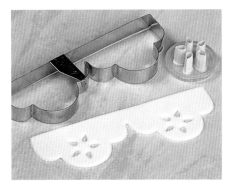

Cut the frill with cutter B and the eyelets with the 5-hole cutter.

INSERTING RIBBON

Broderie anglaise is often threaded with ribbon, and the effect can also be used in cake decorating. Flowerpaste or gelatine paste produces firm pieces of *faux* ribbon that are easy to handle and keep in place.

Roll your chosen paste very thinly and cut it into strips with a sharp knife. Cut the strips into 2cm (^{3}/4in) pieces and drape them over a piece of dowel to dry. When they are ready, cut slits wide enough to insert the ribbon at regular intervals all around the top of the cake, just in from the broderie anglaise. Carefully push a piece of 'ribbon' into alternating pairs of slits and press firmly into place.

Attach a frill of broderie anglaise to the very edge of the tablecloth.

Add a narrower frill of broderie anglaise to create a double layer.

chocolate wedding cake

This chocolate extravaganza is every chocoholic's dream: the inside cake is a very rich chocolate mud cake, the marzipan is secured with a layer of chocolate buttercream, the cake is coated with chocolate sugarpaste (rolled fondant) and the roses are made from a brand new product – chocolate marzipan. Chocolate heaven!

CAKE AND DECORATION

- 30cm (12in), 25cm (10in), 20cm (8in) and 15cm (6in) round chocolate mud cakes (see page 113) or any firm chocolate sponge
- 1kg (2lb) chocolate buttercream (see page 112) or sieved boiled apricot jam
- 5kg (10lb) marzipan
- 41cm (16in) and 28cm (11in) round cake boards
- 20cm (8in) and 15cm (6in) thin, firm, round cake boards
- 5.5kg (11lb) chocolate sugarpaste (rolled fondant) (R)
- 1.5kg (3lb) chocolate marzipan (SK) for 12 roses and leaves
- 750g (1¹/₂lb) dark chocolate buttons (SK)

ESSENTIAL EQUIPMENT

- 12 plastic dowels (cut to the depth of each cake)
- 'A' Baber frill cutter (AB) or template (page 124)
- 3-hole eyelet cutter (PME)
- Greaseproof (parchment) paper piping bags (cones)
- Straight Garrett frill cutter
- Small celstick or paintbrush with a pointed end
- No.44 (star) piping tube (tip) (PME)
- Five 7cm (3in) cake pillars

1 Cover the four cakes with chocolate buttercream or sieved apricot jam. Marzipan the cakes, then place them on either spare cake boards or clean trays. Leave the cakes for at least 4 days, until they have hardened.

2 Cover both the 41cm (16in) and 28cm (11in) round cake boards with chocolate sugarpaste (rolled fondant). Secure the sugarpaste to the boards with a light brushing of boiled water. You should also cover the 20cm (8in) thin, round board with chocolate sugarpaste. Leave all three cake boards to dry thoroughly.

3 Make 12 large roses from the chocolate marzipan (see page 89). Make some rose leaves with leftover paste. Allow them to dry and firm up.

4 With a little jam or buttercream, secure the two thin cake boards to the corresponding-sized cakes. Then, lightly brush the cakes with a little boiled water and cover all four cakes with the chocolate sugarpaste. While the sugarpaste is still relatively soft, insert the plastic dowels into all the cakes except for the top tier (see page 110). Make sure that they are completely level with the top surface of the cakes.

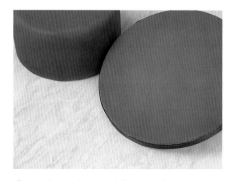

Cover the cakes and the two thicker boards with chocolate sugarpaste.

Secure the cakes to the boards with a small amount of jam or buttercream.

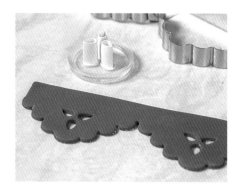

Cut eyelets out of each main frill piece using the 3-hole cutter.

Attach the first piece of broderie anglaise directly to the side of the cake.

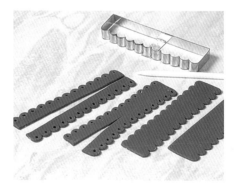

For the top frill, scallop the edges, cut out holes then cut the finished strip in two.

5 Place the 25cm (10in) cake centrally onto the 30cm (12in) cake, and the 15cm (6in) cake onto the 20cm (8in) one. Then, place the two bottom tiers onto the covered 41cm (16in) board, and the two top tiers onto the covered 28cm (11in) board.

6 Put a quarter of the chocolate buttons into a clean basin or bowl, and stand over hot water to melt gently. Keep the melted chocolate on the hot water while you roll out the broderie anglaise pieces.

7 Each Baber frill cutter measures just over 13cm (5in). Measure around the cake and divide the total by the length of the cutter. This will give you the number of frill pieces you require per cake. Invariably, you will not have an exact number, and you may have to insert only a part of the frill. If this is the case, make sure that this odd section is located at the back of the cake. Alternatively, you can cover it up with a part of the floral arrangement.

8 Roll the sugarpaste very thin and cut out the required number of frills, one cake at a time. Then cut out eyelets.

9 Fill a small greaseproof (parchment) piping bag (cone) with melted chocolate. Pipe on enough chocolate to secure one frill at a time, otherwise the chocolate will have set before you are ready to pick up the second piece. Attach the frills directly to the side of the cake. Butt each of the frills up against each other but do not let them overlap.

10 To make the top frill, roll out the sugarpaste very thinly and, with a straight Garrett frill cutter, cut out half the number of frills originally used on the cake. Each frill should be half the width of the actual cutter so one cut will produce two frills. Once cut, each frill should have one straight side and one scalloped side. Turn the cutter around and cut out some scallops on the straight side as well so both sides of the frill are scalloped. With a small celstick or the end of a paintbrush, make some small holes just inside each scallop. Then, cut the piece in half, to obtain two top frills. Finally, attach the two pieces with some melted chocolate, slightly higher than the top line of the main frill. Ensure that the finished frill is in line with the top edge of the cake.

11 Melt some more chocolate, add a little water to thicken it and pipe around the outside edge of all the frills, including the eyelet holes. Pipe either a fine snail trail or some small pearls at the very top edge. Note that you will not require any tube (tip) for the piping at this stage. However, the hole you cut at the end of the piping bag should be small. As chocolate sets very quickly, ensure that you have a sufficient supply of bags to hand, so the chocolate you pipe is always free flowing.

12 Place the remaining chocolate in the bowl, melt and add a little water to thicken. Use more water than in the previous step as the chocolate needs to be thicker this time in order to hold its shape. Fit a larger piping bag with a star tube no.44 and pipe a neat shell border around the base of all the cakes. For the 30cm (12in) and 20cm (8in) cakes, pipe between the cake and the board. With the other two, pipe between cakes.

13 Arrange three marzipan roses and leaves on the top tier of the cake, securing them with a little melted chocolate.

14 Place the 20cm (8in) cake board centrally on the 25cm (10in) cake, and arrange the pillars on the board. Place the remaining nine roses and leaves around the outside top edge of the 25cm (10in) cake. Stack the top two cakes in position. If desired, arrange your choice of ribbons around the base of all the cakes, just above the chocolate shells.

15 This is a semi-stacked cake, so it will not be heavy to transport as it can be carried in two pieces. It would be preferable to assemble the cake at the place of the reception. If you are unable to do it yourself, brief the catering manager thoroughly or provide him with a sketch of how you would like the cake displayed. It would be a shame if, after such hard work, your cake was assembled the wrong way around!

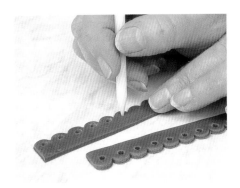

Make holes inside each of the scallops with a celstick or the end of a paintbrush.

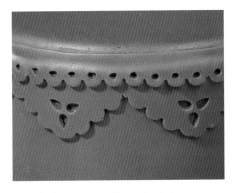

Attach the top frill with melted chocolate, leaving a clear view of the eyelets.

Pipe chocolate shells around the base of the cake with the no.44 star tube.

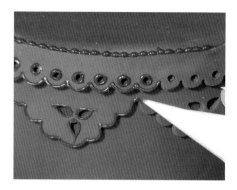

Pipe around all the holes and outside edges with slightly thickened chocolate.

If desired, paint each of the pillars with a dark brown paste food colouring.

Place the pillars between the two tiers of cake before adding the marzipan roses.

sugarcraft tips

• For more control over chocolate for piping, melt it over hot water rather than in a microwave. Always keep it standing over the hot water so it stays liquid. Water or steam thickens the chocolate.

• Cover the pieces of broderie anglaise with a sheet of plastic to prevent them from drying out. The thinner you roll out sugarpaste, the quicker it will dry out. In very warm weather, wipe a smear of white fat or oil onto the sheet of plastic before laying it onto the paste cut-outs.

• When rolling out sugarpaste, keep your working area lightly and frequently dusted with icing sugar. Also, keep manipulating the paste by picking it up with the rolling pin. Do not pick up the paste with your hands, but if you must, make sure to hold your hands very flat.

• Store any leftover piping chocolate in a clean plastic bag. You can use it to grate over trifles and ice creams.

• If you do not have an eyelet cutter, use the end of a paintbrush to create an oval hole by gently it moving up and down.

• Instead of piping around the base of the cakes, you could attach a ribbon or a sugarpaste cord.

CHOCOLATE MARZIPAN

To make chocolate marzipan, knead together equal quantities of white marzipan and Cocoform modelling chocolate.

CHOCOLATE MARZIPAN ROSES

These large, edible roses weigh about 100g (4oz) each. Chocolate marzipan is very pliable, so you can tweak the petals 3 days after they have been made if you are not pleased with their appearance.

1 Take a piece of chocolate marzipan about the size of a small walnut and roll it into a ball. Then, with the outside edges of your hand, roll it into a cone. Stand it upright.

2 Take two pieces of chocolate marzipan about the size of a large grape. Starting in the centre, press and flatten the paste using an outward motion, but only three-quarters of the way around the piece as the petal needs a thick base. Make the paste gradually thinner towards the outside edge of the petal. To make it really thin, either place it in the palm of your hand or on a celpad, and stroke quite firmly using an outward motion with the back of a teaspoon.

3 Wrap the first petal around half of the cone, with the tip of the cone tucked down, as it is not meant to be seen on the finished rose. Place the second petal inside the first, then fold it completely over the cone. With your fingers, work in the petals together at the base of the flower. Before adding the next layer, trim 5mm (1/4in) off the base to prevent the build-up of a thick wedge of paste when assembling the petals.

4 Continue the sequence of petals, ensuring that each row is larger than its predecessor as it is tucked inside it. When the second layer is in place, slightly bend back each petal to give a realistic appearance. Repeat this process with the final layer. Each full-blown rose should have ten petals, assembled in a 2 + 3 + 5 sequence. Once the rose is completed, cut its base on an angle.

CHOCOLATE MARZIPAN LEAVES

1 Roll out the paste quite thinly, about 2.5mm (1/8in) thick and, with a sharp knife, cut out a leaf shape.

2 Place the leaf between two sheets of plastic and, with a teaspoon, stroke the edges in an outward motion. Remove the leaf from the plastic and vein, using the back of a small, sharp knife. Transfer the leaf to a clean surface, and bend it into a fluid shape. Allow to set.

Start with a ball of paste, thin it out with your fingers and bend back each petal.

To attach the petals, a firm squeeze is enough to make them stick.

Cut out the rough shape of the leaf, thin the edges with a spoon and mark veins.

delphinium blues

In this original blue display, the sides of each cake are royal-iced in a different shade of delphinium blue. The blue hues are enhanced in the flower spikes, which are arranged on the bottom tier. Try using a swan stand for this creation, as it provides a true aura of grace to the display.

CAKE AND DECORATION

- 25cm (10in), 20cm (8in) and 15cm (6in) round fruit cakes
- 3kg (6lb) marzipan
- Iris, mid-blue and lavender powder food colourings (EA)
- 35cm (14in), 25cm (10in) and 20cm (8in) round cake boards
- 2kg (4lb) sugarpaste (rolled fondant)
- 2kg (4lb) royal icing
- Painting solution (EA)
- 3 spikes of silk or sugar delphiniums in various hues
- 2.5m (2³/₄yd) x 1cm (¹/₂in) white ribbon

ESSENTIAL EQUIPMENT

- 28cm (11in), 23cm (9in) and 18cm (7in) circles of card
- Greaseproof (parchment) paper piping bags (cones)
- Nos.1 and 2 piping tubes (tips)
- 'B' Baber frill cutter (AB)
- Straight Garrett frill cutter
- 5-hole eyelet cutter (PME)
- Celstick
- 3 posy picks

1 Marzipan the three cakes as for royal icing (see page 105). Allow them to dry for 4 to 5 days.

2 Prepare some royal icing, reserve a small amount of white and divide the remainder into three bowls, one bowl for each cake. Make sure that the amount in each bowl is proportionate to the size of the cake. Colour the largest amount with the lavender food colouring, the second largest with the iris and the third amount

mid-blue with a touch of lavender. Always mix the powder food colourings with a little water to dissolve them into a paste before adding them to either icing or sugarpaste, otherwise you run the risk of speckling. The coloured icing will become darker when dry, so bear this in mind when adding any colour, whether it be liquid, paste or powder. I suggest you practise on a card first.

3 Cover the sides of each cake with at least two coats of royal icing. If desired, apply a third coat. Allow the first coat to dry thoroughly before adding the second. Once both coats are dry, ice the cake boards.

4 Roll out some sugarpaste (rolled fondant) to a 3mm (¹/₈in) thickness and slightly larger than the top of each cake. Brush the marzipanned top surface of

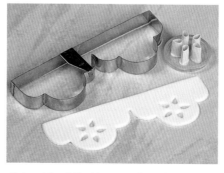

Cut out the frill with cutter B and cut out eyelets with the 5-hole cutter.

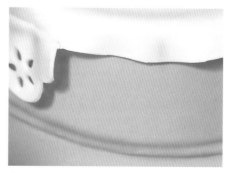

Attach the tablecloth to the cake, then add the frill pieces to the tablecloth.

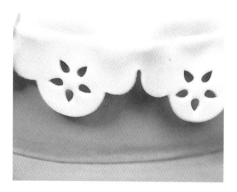

Attach the Baber frill to the very edge of the tablecloth.

For the top frill, cut out scallops, make holes then cut the finished frill in two.

The top frill is attached above the Baber frill once the main frill is secured in place.

the cake with boiled water very sparingly, taking great care not to get any drops of water on the iced surfaces. Pick up the sugarpaste with a rolling pin and place it over the top of the cake. Lightly roll with a pin or a smoother, and trim the edges of the paste to the size of the top of the cake. With the palms of your hands, smooth the edges of the sugarpaste to form a very slight bevel.

5 Roll out some more sugarpaste very thinly. Place one of the circles of card onto the paste and cut around the shape. Remove the card, pick up the paste with a rolling pin and place it over the top of the appropriate cake. Adjust the paste so it is totally even. If the paste has stretched during its transfer, trim it level. Once the paste is correctly positioned, lift up in places and dab on some boiled water so the tablecloth sticks to it. There should be a natural flute to the tablecloth. If not, add some movement from underneath the cloth using your fingers. Leave to set for at least 2 hours.

6 Meanwhile, using a piping bag (cone) fitted with a no.2 tube (tip), pipe some white pearls around the base of each cake.

7 Measure around each cake with the Baber frill to determine how many frills are required per cake. Work on one cake at a time, because the frills are so thin that they will dry out very quickly. Note that the Garrett frill will produce two top frills per cut.

8 Roll out some sugarpaste and cut all the required frills. The frills should be very thin, even thinner than the tablecloth. If they are too thick, they will weigh too much and end up falling off from the sides of the tablecloth. Cover the frills that are not being used immediately with a sheet of plastic. Then, using an eyelet cutter, cut some holes in each Baber frill.

9 Using a piping bag fitted with a no.1 tube, pipe a line of icing to the now firm sugarpaste and start attaching the frill to the very edge of the tablecloth. Use both hands to attach the frill, your left thumb lightly pressing the left edge of the frill onto the tablecloth and your right thumb supporting the centre of the frill, which is the weakest part. Of course, interchange hands if you are left-handed. Do not pull the paste at all costs, otherwise you will distort the eyelet holes as well as the shape of the frill. Always start at the back of the cake to allow an odd piece of frill to be inserted without spoiling the overall appearance of the cake.

10 Attach the top frill with some royal icing, about 5mm (1/4in) above the broderie anglaise frill. By the time you have attached the frills on all three cakes, the frills on the first cake will be firm enough to overpipe. Using a small piping bag fitted with a no.1 tube, pipe around the edge of both frills, including the eyelets. When piping around the eyelets, the tube should be touching the surface of the cake. Pipe the petal shape of the eyelet one half at a time to achieve a better result. Then, pipe a very small snail trail around the top edge of the frill. This piping should look like small and neat stitches.

11 Select one or two flowers from each spike (if using silk), and place them on the surface of the two smaller cakes. Push the three posy picks into the base of the largest cake, and arrange the delphiniums. Use a whole flowerhead, or pick off the petals and scatter them.

12 Attach the ribbons around the cake boards.

Pipe pearls around the base of each of the cakes using the no.2 tube.

Pipe around the holes, eyelets and scalloped edges.

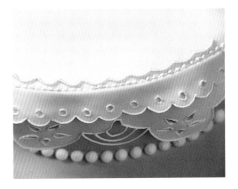

Try piping small iced scallops in double lines around the top edge of the frill.

sugarcraft tips

- On the top edge of the frills you can pipe small, neat scallops. Start the line with a no.1 tube, then overpipe with a no.1 and then no.0 tube, the latter in either white or a matching colour. Pipe string lines in the centre of the frill using a no.1 tube.

- If you choose to make the cakes white instead of blue, use a coloured icing to pipe around the eyelets and the top scallops.

- Instead of making scallops around the top edge, use a crimper and overpipe. However, make sure the paste is scalloped as soon as the tablecloth is placed onto the cake, otherwise it would be too dry.

lisianthus tablecloth

One simple way of creating a cloth effect on a cake is to throw over a piece of sugarpaste and let it hang over the edge. A popular flower at the moment is the lisianthus, which ranges from white to pale and deep purple. The piping is kept to a minimum and echoes the floral spray to give a light, airy feel to the cake.

CAKE AND DECORATION

- 25cm (10in) round, rich fruit cake
- 1.5kg (3lb) marzipan
- 1kg (2lb) royal icing
- Violet paste food colouring (W)
- 36cm (14in) round cake board
- 1kg (2lb) sugarpaste (rolled fondant)
- Lisianthus blooms and 6 to 8 buds and leaves (silk or sugar)
- 90cm (3ft) x 1cm (1/2in) deep purple ribbon
- 1.2m (4ft) x 1cm (1/2in) pale lilac ribbon

ESSENTIAL EQUIPMENT

- 33cm (13in) circle of card
- Sharp knife
- Straight Garrett frill cutter
- Bulbous tool (PME)
- Greaseproof (parchment) paper piping bags (cones)
- No.1 piping tube (tip)

1 Marzipan the cake as for royal icing (see page 105). Allow to dry for a few days.

2 Make some royal icing and reserve some white. Colour the rest with the violet paste food colouring and ice the sides of the cake at least twice – three times would be ideal. Once the sides are dry, ice the cake board.

3 Roll out half the amount of sugarpaste (rolled fondant) and cover the top of the cake, securing it to the marzipan with a little boiled water. Trim off the sides and smooth the edges with the palms of your hands to create a slight bevel.

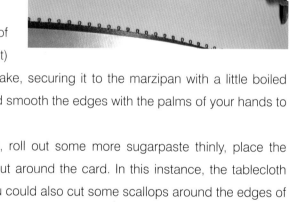

4 To make the tablecloth, roll out some more sugarpaste thinly, place the circle of card onto it and cut around the card. In this instance, the tablecloth has been kept plain but you could also cut some scallops around the edges of the cloth. You would then pipe the edges of each scallop, using a no.1 or 0 piping tube (tip).

Place the tablecloth onto the prepared cake so that it is even all the way around.

Cut out white and purple pieces of sugarpaste using the Garrett frill cutter.

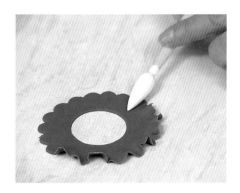

Frill each of the cut-out pieces using the bulbous tool.

Stages for attaching the frills: attach purple pieces first and white on top.

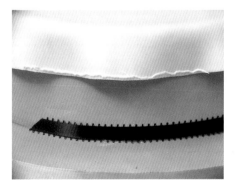

Pipe royal icing onto the very edge of the tablecloth ready to attach the Garrett frill.

5 Pick up the paste with a rolling pin and position it on the top of the cake so it falls evenly all the way around. To adjust the cloth, slip your fingers under the paste and move it around. Once the tablecloth is in position, lift it up in places and brush some boiled water onto the top of the cake to secure the cloth. Allow to firm for a few hours.

6 Using the violet paste food colouring, colour enough sugarpaste to make seven Garrett frills. Roll out the sugarpaste thinly, cut out the seven Garrett frills and cover with a sheet of plastic. With the bulbous tool, frill the cut-outs one at a time. Fit a piping bag (cone) with a no.1 tube and fill with royal icing. With a line of royal icing, attach the frills to the edge of the tablecloth. Make sure each frill is closely butted to its neighbour, not overlapping it. When the first row is completed, use a bulbous tool to lift the frills every 4cm (1¹/2in) to give them movement.

7 Repeat the above process, this time using the white sugarpaste. Ensure that you attach each white frill exactly on top of the under-frill, this time allowing them to overlap slightly. In order to hide the join, lift the edge of the frill and curl it under a little.

8 When all the frills are in place, use a no.1 tube to pipe either some small pearls or a snail trail where the frills join the tablecloth. Then, pipe some large, random 'S' and 'C' scrolls all over the surface of the tablecloth. You can also pipe cornelli work, if preferred.

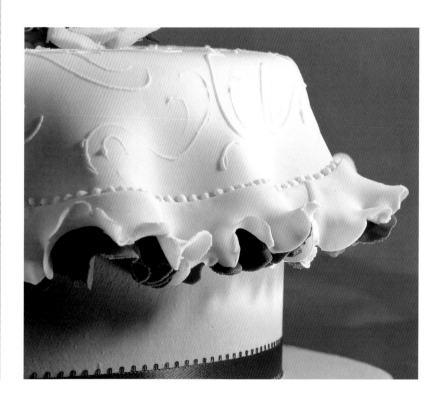

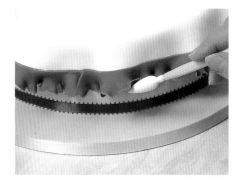

Lift the frills up every so often with the bulbous tool to give them movement.

9 Arrange the lisianthus in a 'C'-shape, and attach it to the top of the cake with a piece of sugarpaste and some royal icing. As this is a rather heavy bouquet, it will probably need support from small pieces of foam or polystyrene until it is dry.

10 Place the deep purple ribbon around the base of the cake and secure it with a thin line of icing. Finally, attach the pale lilac ribbon to the cake board.

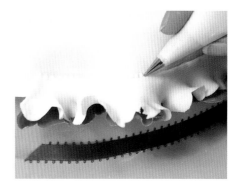

Once the frills are attached to the cake, neaten the edges with a tiny snail trail.

sugarcraft tips

• Instead of piping, you can roll the tablecloth with an embossed pin (see page 10) before placing it onto the cake. If you choose this option, you will only need to make a single Garrett frill, of the same colour as the cloth.

• Try piping some refined embroidery patterns onto the tablecloth to obtain a delicate finish.

• If preferred, replace the ribbon at the base of the cake with a white Garrett frill, flowing all the way around the cake and resting on the cake board. Secure the frill with a little icing.

• If lisianthus are not readily available, substitute them with violets. Violets are smaller flowers, but they will certainly convey a feeling of freshness to the cake as well as keeping in with the purple and white colour scheme.

Pipe large 'S' and 'C' scrolls freehand all across the tablecloth surface.

pretty in pink

This pretty pink cake is an innovative creation as it features a new daisy cutter. My main goal was to match the design to the delicate look of the flowers. The floral bouquet, in its glass flower vase, echoes the Victorian tradition of preserving bridal bouquets for posterity and provides the cake with a hint of old-fashion quaintness.

CAKE AND DECORATION

- 25cm (10in), 20cm (8in) and 15cm (6in) round, rich fruit cakes, 9cm (3½in) deep
- 3.5kg (7lb) marzipan
- 4kg (8lb) sugarpaste (rolled fondant)
- 100g (4oz) flowerpaste
- Pink and egg yellow paste food colourings (Spectral)
- 1kg (2lb) royal icing
- Icing (powdered) sugar
- 7.5cm (3in) and 13cm (5in) thin, round boards
- 15cm (6in) tall, glass vase
- Mixed bouquet of salmon pink daisies, foliage and other small flowers (silk or sugar)
- 1.75m (2yd) x 1cm (½in) white ribbon

ESSENTIAL EQUIPMENT

- 2.5cm (1in) and 2cm (¾in) daisy cutters (PME)
- Ball tool
- Grater
- Flower stand (OP)
- 'F' Baber frill cutter (AB)
- 3 circles of foam, 2.5cm (1in) smaller than top of each cake
- 3 cake boards or stiff cards, same size as circles of foam
- Greaseproof (parchment) paper piping bags (cones)
- Nos.1 and 2 piping tubes (tips)

1 Marzipan the cakes and leave to dry for 4 to 5 days. Cover the cakes with white sugarpaste (rolled fondant), and leave for a further 4 days.

2 Colour the majority of the flowerpaste salmon pink, using the pink paste food colouring mixed with a touch of yellow. Colour the remainder yellow.

3 Roll out the salmon pink flowerpaste very thinly and, with daisy cutters, cut out

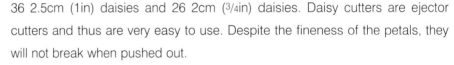

36 2.5cm (1in) daisies and 26 2cm (¾in) daisies. Daisy cutters are ejector cutters and thus are very easy to use. Despite the fineness of the petals, they will not break when pushed out.

4 Elongate the petals slightly with the ball tool and gently pinch each petal to a point. Attach the two layers of petals together with a little royal icing, placing the second set inside and in-between the other. The petals are arranged in the following manner: stick two layers of smaller petals for the daisies on the top tier; an outer layer of larger daisy petals and inner layer of smaller ones for the middle tier; and two layers of larger petals for the bottom tier.

5 Once the petals are completed, take the small piece of yellow flowerpaste and press it into the smallest hole of a grater. Then, place the ball in the centre

Cut out and assemble the daisies in advance, then leave them to dry.

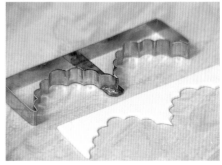

Cut out the broderie anglaise frill using the 'F' Baber frill cutter.

Cut out double rows of frills for the top and bottom of the cake side.

Attach the bottom frills first, securing them with a small amount of royal icing.

Next, attach the top row of frills, making sure it aligns with the bottom row.

of each daisy, securing it with a little royal icing. Transfer the daisies to a flower stand to dry. This will create daisies with a slightly cupped appearance. Leave to dry thoroughly.

6 Roll out some sugarpaste thinly and, with the 'F' Baber frill cutter, cut out enough frills to go around the top and base of each cake. Working on one cake at a time, secure the frills into place with royal icing. When all three cakes have been completed, place the circular piece of foam in the centre of its respective cake, one cake at a time. Then, place the board or card on the foam and turn the cake upside down.

7 For ease of piping and to make the loops fall perfectly straight, the cake needs to be placed at eye level. Therefore, transfer the cake onto a turntable and then onto something else to lift it even higher.

8 Fit a piping bag (cone) with a no.1 tube (tip), fill with royal icing and pipe around the scallops in the top pieces of broderie anglaise frill – which are now upside down. Also pipe some crossed-over loops, making them touch the edge of the frill. Leave to dry at least 20 minutes before turning the cake the correct way up. Pipe all three cakes using the same process.

9 Pipe around the scallops on the bottom frill. Then, pipe a dot at the base of each loop and tiny clusters of three dots, hardly applying any pressure, over the entire surface of the frills. Using a no.2 tube, pipe some delicate pearls around the base of each cake.

10 Add a little icing (powdered) sugar to the royal icing to make it slightly stiffer than the piping icing. Attach the daisies to the cake, according to size, securing them with the stiffer icing. This will prevent the flowers from sliding.

11 Cover both thin boards with sugarpaste, and only leave the smaller one to dry overnight. On the larger one, stick on a small amount of sugarpaste and arrange the flowers accordingly. Measure the height of the flower arrangement against that of the vase, then place the vase over the flowers and press it into the sugarpaste covering the board. The sugarpaste should still be soft and thus the vase soon creates a rim in which it will sit nicely once the paste has thoroughly dried. In this way, both the vase and the floral arrangement will be held firm, and be safe for travelling. Arrange the remaining flowers to the top tier.

12 Attach the ribbons around the bases of the cake boards.

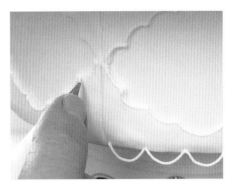

Turn the cake upside down and pipe along the scalloped edge of the frills.

Drop the first row of piped loops and then drop another row, criss-crossing the first.

Attach the daisies in the centre of the spaces between the frills.

sugarcraft tips

• When piping, never push the icing uphill as it will curl up into little balls. You can pull it sideways and down, or loop it downwards.

• Instead of using a flower stand, try inserting the daisy onto a thick piece of foam and pressing the small end of the ball tool down into centre of the flower.

• The vase used for this particular recipe was a cheap one. However, you can use a more expensive one as long as it is well secured. The vase could be a gift from you to the newly-weds. The vase doubles up as an excellent container to preserve the flowers if you choose to make them in sugar.

• If preferred, you can make this cake using royal icing all over instead of sugarpaste. If you choose the royal icing option, make sure the Baber frills are attached to the sides of the cake with royal icing instead of boiled water.

engagement celebration

This cake has been designed to celebrate an engagement. The strong green colour symbolizes the strength of the union of the young couple sitting on the bench with their arms entwined. The grapes are a toast to their good health and happiness, and the stark white of both the sugarpaste and royal icing epitomizes the purity of love.

CAKE AND DECORATION

- 30cm (12in) round, rich fruit cake
- 2kg (4lb) marzipan
- 2.25kg (4¹/2lb) dark green and 500g (1lb) white sugarpaste (rolled fondant)
- 41cm (16in) round cake board
- 500g (1lb) royal icing
- Violet (W), black, Christmas green and pink paste food colourings (Spectral)
- Top ornament (FARO 211)
- 1.25m (1¹/2yd) x 1cm (¹/2in) dark green ribbon

ESSENTIAL EQUIPMENT

- 'A' Baber frill cutter (AB)
- Ruler
- Sharp knife
- Greaseproof (parchment) paper piping bags (cones)
- Nos.1 and 1.5 piping tubes (tips)
- Circle of foam
- Cake board or stiff card, same size as circle of foam

1 Marzipan the cake and leave it to dry for a couple of days.

2 Roll out some green sugarpaste (rolled fondant) very thinly and cover the cake board. Allow the board to dry. Cover the cake with the green sugarpaste and place it onto the cake board. Leave the cake to dry.

3 Measure around the side of the cake and calculate how many frills need to be cut out. Cut the required number of frills. Then, with a ruler, trim 5mm (¹/4in) off the straight side of each frill.

4 Fill a piping bag (cone) with some royal icing and, helping yourself with a ruler, pipe dots of icing to form a line around the exact centre of the cake. Attach the frills, making sure that the straight sides are butted together, that each frill is in line with its neighbour and that the edges are along the marked centre line.

5 Colour the royal icing, first mixing in some violet paste food colouring, then adding minute amounts of red and black until you obtain the required shade. Also colour some of the icing green to make the leaves and vines.

6 Using the template on page 118, pipe the grapes with a no.1 tube (tip) and, making the first four grapes in a slight downward curve. Continue piping the

Trim the pieces of broderie anglaise slightly, unless the cake is very deep.

Attach the bottom frill first of all, using a small amount of royal icing.

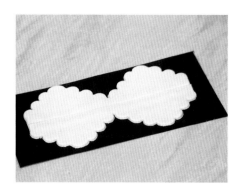

The two pieces of broderie anglaise butted together.

Pipe the grapes and leaf design onto the broderie pieces.

Practise piping around the scalloped-edge frills before applying to the cake.

grapes in a graduating diamond shape, leaving only one grape at the tip. Return to the top of the bunch and pipe more grapes until you build up a realistic heap. Make sure the icing is stiff enough so the grapes do not appear to blend into each other but show up separately.

7 Divide the green icing into two piping bags, one fitted with a no.1 tube (tip) and the other tubeless. With the first bag, pipe the vines along the joining line, so the line hardly shows when you have finished. Then, take the second bag, press the tip firmly between your finger and thumb and cut an inverted 'V' shape (see page 118). Use this bag to pipe the leaves.

8 Place a piece of foam on top of the cake, then add a cake board or a stiff piece of card on top of the foam. Turn the cake upside down and pipe around the scalloped edge of the frill. Moving outwards, pipe two more lines directly onto the cake. Finally, pipe even rows of five dots.

9 Turn the cake the correct way up, and repeat the piping on the bottom edge of the frill, continuing down onto the cake board.

10 Attach the ornament slightly off-centre on the cake, in order to leave room for either some scroll piping (used here) or a written message of your choice. Use a no.1.5 tube to pipe the first lines of scroll piping, directly onto the cake. Overpipe using the same tube, then pipe the final line with a no.1 tube.

11 Attach the ribbon around the cake board.

sugarcraft tips

• Alternative colour combinations could be brown and cream, or two shades of pink. Use a red, white and green colour scheme for a Christmas cake, while a white and blue combination would suit a christening cake perfectly.

• When rolling out a dark-coloured sugarpaste, try to prevent the appearance of sugar patches on the coloured surface. To do this, first mix some icing (powdered) sugar into the paste, then make sure there is sufficient icing on the surface of your working area. When rolling the paste, keep the paste moving to prevent sticking. If the rolling pin needs to be dusted, take it away from the paste and lightly sprinkle with icing sugar. Wipe off the excess with your hand.

basic techniques and recipes

TECHNIQUES

ROYAL ICING

Royal icing is a mixture of icing (powdered) sugar and egg white, combined in the correct proportions, beaten (not whisked) for the correct length of time and at the correct speed to achieve an icing of perfection. With a perfect icing, the surfaces of a marzipanned cake can be iced with barely a blemish, and you can create piped work of such delicacy that it looks almost impossible for human hands to have had any part in its creation. Royal icing is set when it is firm enough to hold any shape it is given. It can then travel safely under reasonable conditions and should hold two or three tiers of cake without sinking and yet still be able to be cut without having to be resort to a hacksaw.

marzipanning a cake for royal icing

When constructing anything from a house to a cake, it is easier to progress to a perfect finish if the foundations are sound and true. Therefore, make sure that the sides of the cake are perfectly straight and form a 90 degree angle on the top edge. Thankfully, most modern cake tins are accurately made, but you may need to cut the cake a little in order to straighten the sides and top, especially if the top has risen during baking.

1 Thinly spread some sieved apricot jam on the top of the cake only.

2 Roll out two-thirds of the marzipan until it is about 5mm (1/4in) thick and 2.5cm (1in) larger than the cake. Always keep the underside of the marzipan well dusted with icing sugar to prevent it from sticking.

3 Put the top of the cake onto the marzipan and cut around the shape of the cake. Pick up the cake marzipan-side-up and set aside.

4 Roll the rest of the marzipan, with the trimmings, into a strip long enough to go around the whole cake. Dust the work surface and roll out the paste evenly. The strip should be slightly deeper than the cake.

5 Trim off each end of the strip and cut straight along one side only. Then, roll up like a bandage and stand upright, cut-side-down.

6 Dust the work surface again and place the cake marzipanned-side-down onto it. Spread some jam sparingly around the sides of the cake.

Trim the strip of marzipan along three sides only.

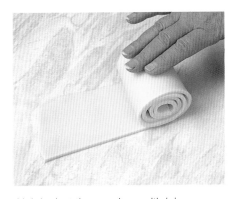

Lightly dust the marzipan with icing sugar and roll up like a bandage.

Unroll the 'bandage' around the sides of the ready-jammed cake, cut-side-down.

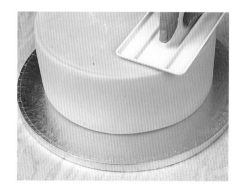

Smooth the top and side edges of the marzipan to keep the 90 degree angle.

Allow the marzipan to harden for at least 4 to 5 days before icing the cake.

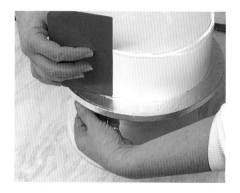

Once the sides are iced, use a scraper to smooth and even out the icing.

7 Unroll the 'bandage' around the cake, cutting off any surplus where the two ends meet. With a sharp knife, trim off the surplus marzipan on what will be the bottom of the cake. Place the cake right-side-up in the middle of the cake board, then smooth the top and sides of the marzipan with a smoother. You will now have a 90 degree edge to the top of your cake, which is ready for the first coat of royal icing. The cake should be left for at least 4 to 5 days for the marzipan to harden before it is royal iced – a little longer in damp or humid conditions.

marzipanning tips

- In the days when all celebration cakes were royal iced, many bakers used a spirit level to ensure the exactness of the top and sides.
- Cakes must always be cold before marzipanning as the combination of sweet jam, enzymes in the marzipan and heat can cause fermentation and ultimately bacterial spoilage.

royal icing a cake

To make a perfect royal icing, use 3.5kg (7lb) icing (powdered) sugar and 0.5l (1pint/2¹/₂cups) of egg white. For a smaller quantity, the ratio is 210g (7oz) icing sugar to 35ml (1¹/₄oz) egg white. For reference, 1 fresh egg white (grade 2 egg) weighs about 30g (1oz). You can also use 90g (3oz) powdered egg white reconstituted with 0.5l (1pint/ 2¹/₂ cups) cold water.

1 Sieve the total amount of icing (powdered) sugar into a machine bowl and pour in the egg white. It is important to initially blend in the ingredients by hand.

2 Beat on medium speed until the icing stands in a peak. To test, dip a palette knife into the mixture, draw it out and hold it upright. If the sugar does not flop over, then the consistency is correct.

3 To ice a cake successfully you will need to use a turntable, a firm, straight-sided plastic scraper and a solid palette knife. A royal-iced cake should have at least two coats of icing. Wait until the first coat is perfectly dry before applying the second layer.

4 To apply the royal icing, first spread it around the sides of the cake with the palette knife, paddling backwards and forwards on each new application to get rid of air bubbles. When the sides are completely covered, use the scraper to smooth and even out the icing.

5 To ice the top of the cake, smooth the icing onto the surface with the palette knife. Paddle the knife backwards and forwards, moving the cake around on the turntable to work out any air bubbles. Then, with the back of the long-bladed knife, hold each end firmly, laying it almost flat onto the edge of the cake and pull it towards you in a single motion.

6 Clean off the edges with the palette knife, making sure to keep the 90 degree angle. If you prefer a bevelled edge, lay the knife at an angle on the edge of the cake and hold it there, while turning the cake a full circle.

royal icing a cake board

Ice the cake board after you have applied the second coat to the cake. This can be achieved in two ways. One way is to spread the royal icing around the board with a small palette knife, then hold the knife almost flat on the surface and hold the underside of the turntable to swing the whole thing around with one continuous motion. Alternatively, the board can be iced before the cake is positioned on it. Use royal icing that has had a little water added, thus allowing it to flow over the surface of the board more easily. Smooth with a large palette knife or a steel ruler. Bang sharply to bring any air bubbles to the surface.

royal icing tips

- When making up royal icing, always make sure the bowl, beater, wooden spoon and egg whites are grease free. The presence of greases will prevent the egg white from incorporating any air.
- If using powdered egg white, check with your supplier what type you have because some brands need 24 hours to reconstitute.
- Add a few drops of blue food colouring during beating to produce snow-white royal icing.

Pull the back of a long-bladed knife across the icing with one motion.

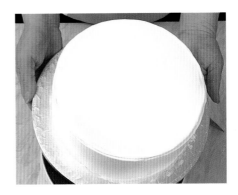

Clean off the edges with a small-bladed palette knife, keeping the 90 degree angle.

Once the royal icing has set thoroughly, piping can commence.

Using a rolling pin, lift the marzipan onto the jam-covered cake in one piece.

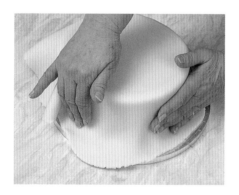

Use both hands to ease the marzipan into the base and work out any folds.

Trim off any surplus marzipan with the point of a sharp knife.

MARZIPANNING A CAKE FOR SUGARPASTE (ROLLED FONDANT)

The 'bevelled' edge look is a very popular design for sugarpaste cakes. It enables the marzipan to be positioned over the cake in one piece. However, just as much care needs to be taken with the smoothness of the surface of the cake, otherwise a lumpy texture will be visible even through the final coating of the sugarpaste.

Marzipan should always be firmly attached to the cake. It is usually best to use boiled and sieved apricot jam, as it will not show a line of colour should any seepage occur.

1 Make sure that the top surface of the cake is totally flat, and trim if necessary.

2 Measure the cake from the base, over the top, and back down to the base on the opposite side. This will ensure that enough marzipan is rolled out to cover the cake comfortably in one piece without patching. If soft tape is not available, a piece of string will do the job equally well.

3 Roll out the marzipan to about a 5mm (1/4in) thickness. Try to keep it in a circular shape if coating a round cake. Then, brush the cake with sieved apricot jam if using a fruit cake or smooth over buttercream if using a sponge.

4 Pick up the marzipan with a rolling pin and, starting at the front, ease it over the entire surface of the cake. Using your hands, ease the marzipan into the base of the cake, smoothing any folds as you work around the cake.

5 With a sharp knife, trim off any surplus marzipan. Then, with the back of the knife, push the remainder tightly into the base of the cake where it meets the board. Re-trim if necessary.

6 Should any cracking occur on the top edge of the marzipan, rub briskly with the palm of your hand. This method can also be used to remove cracks from the sugarpaste itself and, if you smear your palm with a tiny amount of vegetable fat, the disappearance of cracks from the sugarpaste is almost total.

7 Before covering with sugarpaste, first brush the marzipan with boiled water. The technique for covering with sugarpaste is exactly the same as for covering with marzipan.

RE-USABLE MOULDING GEL

With agar-agar as its main ingredient, re-usable moulding gel is probably one of the most useful and versatile products to come onto the market recently. Moulding gel makes it possible to form your own moulds from a wide variety of objects, which gives both the amateur and the professional cake decorator enormous scope to adorn their cakes with original pieces. You can make two- or three-dimensional moulds, though three-dimensional ones will obviously require more gel. Moulds can be made using buttons, jewellery (particularly brooches), plastic animals and leaves, fridge magnets, small ornaments made from china, plastic, wood or metal and coins, while fresh leaves from the garden enable you to make your own leaf veiners.

The fact that it can be used over and over again makes the gel all the more popular. If you are not entirely satisfied with the end result or have made a mistake, you simply cut up the gel, re-melt it and try again. It also means that if you need to make a one-off mould, such as a frog or a teapot, provided you can find a prototype, you will never be left with a mould that will probably be used only once.

1 Create a container from non-toxic plasticine or foil, or use an existing plastic container to hold your chosen object. It is essential that the container is a good 2.5cm (1in) deeper than the object. If you are using plasticine, first roll it out then make a snug-fitting cup by placing the object presentation-side-up in the centre, then working around it to lift the sides up, pinching to form a firm container. Use the same method for making a foil container. Place the finished container onto a table mat or small board to ensure everything stays level when the mould is carried to the refrigerator or freezer.

2 Take the lid off a 250g (8oz) pot of moulding gel and melt very gently in a microwave with the power as low as defrost (or even lower if your microwave is particularly powerful). You can also melt the gel over hot water but the process takes longer and you need to take care not to get any water in it as this weakens the gelling properties. Set the microwave initially for 2 minutes, check and repeat with 1 or 2-minute blasts until the gel is almost melted (it will melt from the outside in). Stir gently with a small palette knife. Too much agitation will cause air bubbles to form.

The moulding gel is poured over the object into a plasticine container.

Peel off the plasticine or foil then turn the mould presentation-side-up.

Ease the gel away from the sides of the object to release.

These button moulds were created using moulding gel.

moulding tips

• Moulding gel is food grade and as such it can be used to form a mould for making completely edible pieces.

• Any object made from fabric will not work in the mould as the gel will stick to the fibres. It is well worth experimenting with plastic doilies to make your own lace pieces.

3 Pour the melted, lump-free gel into the container, covering the object completely so that it can no longer be seen. Then, carry the gel-filled container to the refrigerator (or freezer if the object is large and a lot of gel has been used). Leave until the surface of the gel feels quite cold. Peel off the plasticine or foil, then turn the mould over and trim off any excess gel that might have seeped underneath the object. Ease the gel away from the sides of the object to release. Every single marking in your chosen piece should be well defined.

For additional information on the moulding technique, a video demonstrating how to use moulding gel, called *Something Gelled*, is available from Videopoint (see Suppliers on page 125).

BASIC DOWELLING

With the ever-growing popularity of stacked cakes, the need for dowelling will almost certainly arise from time to time.

In my opinion, a stacked royal-iced cake does not need to be dowelled. If the royal icing has been correctly made, the cakes will support each other for two reasons – first, they will be rich fruit cakes, more often than not, and therefore solid enough; and second, if each cake has had a minimum of three coats, it will be sufficient to support the other tiers. If in any doubt, add a little acid in the form of either lemon juice, white vinegar or acetic acid to the icing for the bottom tier in order to strengthen it.

Dowels should not be made of wood. Wood splinters and, since it is a porous material, it cannot be considered hygienic, even if it has been boiled. Modern dowels made from an acceptable plastic material can be purchased from most cake decorating shops.

There are two methods of inserting dowels in cakes, depending upon whether hollow or solid pillars are used.

For hollow pillars:

1 Mark out the position of each hollow pillar and insert the dowels. Each dowel must be the height of a pillar and long enough to go through the cake to the board.

2 Sink the dowel into the cake, then place a pillar over each dowel.

3 Cut each dowel to size with a small hacksaw. Put both the pillars and dowels back into place and check the overall balance. It is essential to ensure that all the cakes are absolutely level – I cannot stress this enough. Once the cake has been delivered to the reception, it will be too late to find that it leans over at an angle.

For solid pillars:

Follow the same steps as for hollow pillars, except that the dowels will need to be cut so they are level with the surface of the cake, rather than the same height as the pillars. With this method, it is important to inform the caterers that plastic rods have been used and provide them with their exact location in the cake.

Dowels are sunk directly in stacked cakes such as this one.

RECIPES

GELATINE PASTE

Gelatine paste has been used in this book for the White and Gold Drape creation (see pages 26–29). In this particular recipe, it is mixed with the flowerpaste in order to provide extra elasticity to the stunning ornamental draping.

The sugarpaste tiles are strengthened with gelatine paste.

- 10ml (2tsp) gelatine powder
- 1 rounded tsp liquid glucose
- 250g (8oz/2cups) icing (powdered) sugar

1 Sprinkle the gelatine onto 15ml (1tbsp) of water. When it has formed a solid cake, stand in very hot – but not boiling – water until the gelatine has completely dissolved and become crystal clear.

2 Add the glucose and stir until it is thoroughly mixed in.

3 Make a well in the icing (powdered) sugar, pour in the liquid ingredients and knead all the ingredients together until you obtain a smooth paste consistency.

4 Cover with cling film and leave the paste for at least half a day before using it.

Mix gelatine paste to the sugarpaste to provide elasticity to the drape.

Mix flowerpaste with sugarpaste to get a harder-setting paste for plaques.

chocolate buttercream

Make the buttercream and pour in 250g (8oz) of dark melted chocolate, beating thoroughly in order to prevent the chocolate from forming into lumps. If using a machine, make sure that the chocolate is poured into the bowl between the beater and the edge of the bowl, otherwise it will cling to the beater.

Use this buttercream to coat the chocolate mud cake before adding the sugarpaste.

FLOWERPASTE

Flowerpaste can be used on its own or mixed in a 50:50 ratio with sugarpaste to give a more elastic paste for drapes, or a harder-setting paste for plaques or tiles.

- Generous 50g (2oz) white vegetable fat
- 15ml (1tbsp) gum tragacanth
- 250g (8oz/2cups) sieved icing (powdered) sugar
- 10ml (2tsp) gelatine
- 1 large egg white (remove string)

1 Grease a bowl with a little white vegetable fat and place the bowl over hot water. Add the gum tragacanth and half the total amount of sugar. Warm to 37˚C (98˚F).

2 Add the gelatine to 15ml (1tbsp) of water and dissolve. Please refer to step 1 of the gelatine paste recipe for how to dissolve the gelatine.

3 Beat the egg white slightly and add to the icing, together with the gelatine. Beat until creamy. Work in the remaining sugar and beat well.

4 Remove from the bowl and work in the vegetable fat. If the finished paste is too soft, add a little more icing; if is too stiff, add a little more egg white. Store in a plastic bag.

BUTTERCREAM

Buttercream has been used in the Pretty Cushion cake (see pages 52–55) to attach the marzipan to the surface of the cake and provide moistness and flavour through the centre of the sponge.

- 500g (1lb/2cups) unsalted butter or margarine
- 420g (14oz/3$\frac{1}{2}$cups) icing (powdered) sugar
- 60g (2oz/$\frac{1}{2}$cup) milk powder
- Vanilla, lemon, orange, coffee and almond flavourings

1 Beat the butter or margarine until it turns light and fluffy.

2 Sieve together the icing (powdered) sugar and milk powder, then gradually beat this mixture into the butter.

3 Once all the dry ingredients have been incorporated, beat in 15ml (1tbsp) of hot water. Add any flavouring as required.

DARK CHOCOLATE MUD CAKE

This is a very rich and beautifully moist chocolate cake. I used this recipe for the Chocolate Patchwork cake and the Chocolate Wedding Cake (see pages 48–51 and 84–89, respectively). Dark chocolate mud cake can be made well in advance and deep frozen, or wrapped in greaseproof (parchment) paper and foil then stored for at least a week to 10 days prior to decorating.

The following recipe is enough to make either a 23cm (9in) square cake 8cm (3½in) deep, or a 25cm (10in) round cake that is slightly shallower. For a 30cm (12in) cake, increase the quantities by half again, for a 20cm (8in) cake, reduce them by a quarter and for a 15cm (6in) cake reduce them by half.

This stunning patchwork cake uses the chocolate mud cake as a base.

- 750g (1½lb/3cups) butter
- 1.2kg (2lb6oz) dark chocolate
- 550g (1lb2oz/2cups) brown sugar
- 35g (1oz/⅓cup) instant coffee granules
- 560ml (22floz) water
- 6 eggs
- 150ml (¼pint/⅔cup) coffee liqueur
- 435g (14½oz/4cups) soft cake flour
- 200g (6½oz/2cups) self-raising flour

1 Line either a 23cm (9in) or a 25cm (10in) cake tin with greaseproof (parchment) paper. Preheat the oven to 130˚C/266˚F/gas mark 1.

2 Gently heat both the butter and the dark chocolate until melted thoroughly, either in a microwave on a very low setting or over a pan of hot water.

3 Combine the brown sugar, coffee and water with the chocolate/butter mix, and beat until smooth.

4 Lightly beat the eggs and add to the coffee liqueur. Then, fold in the soft and self-raising flours.

mud cake tips

- It is best to use a good quality chocolate, one with over 50 per cent cocoa solids – not a 'chocolate flavoured' product.
- Dark chocolate is most often used for this recipe, although white chocolate would work equally well. However, never use milk chocolate as it tends to lump when cooked.

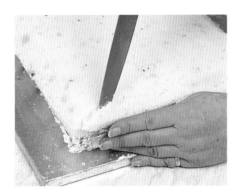

Leave the sponge until it is a day old before attempting to cut it.

Heap the cut-out pieces into the centre of the cake to give a puffed cushion shape.

5 Beat the mixture on a slow speed if you are using a machine, or steadily if using a wooden spoon. Continue beating until the batter is smooth and glossy.

6 Pour the mixture into the ready-lined cake tin and bake for 4 to 5 hours. Test with a skewer, or by gently pressing with your fingers. It is ready when the cake springs back up.

GENOESE SPONGE

This is a firm sponge that can be carved into shapes more easily than some of the lighter sponges. I have used this particular sponge for the Pretty Cushion cake (see pages 52–55), but it could just as well be used for carving out an unusual shape to make any sort of novelty cake. The following recipe makes a 30cm (12in) cake.

• 500g (1lb/2cups) butter (unsalted) or a good quality margarine
• 500g (1lb/2cups) caster (superfine) sugar
• 11 eggs, beaten
• 620g (1lb4oz/5cups) sieved plain (all-purpose) flour

1 Grease and line a 30cm (12in) square cake tin with greaseproof (parchment) paper. Preheat the oven to 160°C/320°F/gas mark 4.

2 Cream together the caster (superfine) sugar and butter or margarine, until you obtain a light and fluffy consistency. It is preferable to use a machine if possible.

3 Gradually beat in the eggs, incorporating each addition thoroughly before adding the next.

4 Fold in the flour and mix thoroughly until you have a smooth batter. Once this has been achieved, add a few drops of flavouring if desired.

5 Pour the mixture into the lined cake tin and bake until firm to the touch – about 1 1/2 hours.

6 Remove the cake from the oven and immediately place the cake upside down onto a cooling wire in order to prevent it from sweating in the tin. Un-mould the cake from the tin, peel off the lining paper and replace it loosely on top of the cake. To store the sponge, wrap it in greaseproof paper.

templates

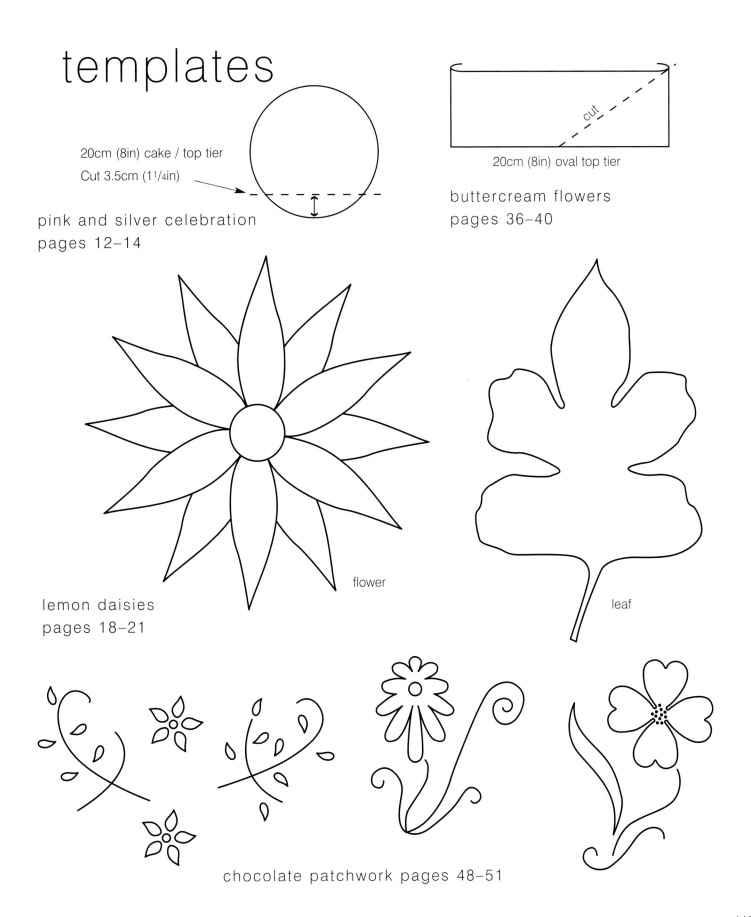

20cm (8in) cake / top tier

Cut 3.5cm (1¼in)

pink and silver celebration
pages 12–14

20cm (8in) oval top tier

buttercream flowers
pages 36–40

cut

flower

leaf

lemon daisies
pages 18–21

chocolate patchwork pages 48–51

chocolate patchwork pages 48–51

folk art cake / side panel ornaments pages 68–71

folk art cake / side panel ornaments pages 68–71

Folk art cake / side panel ornaments pages 68–71

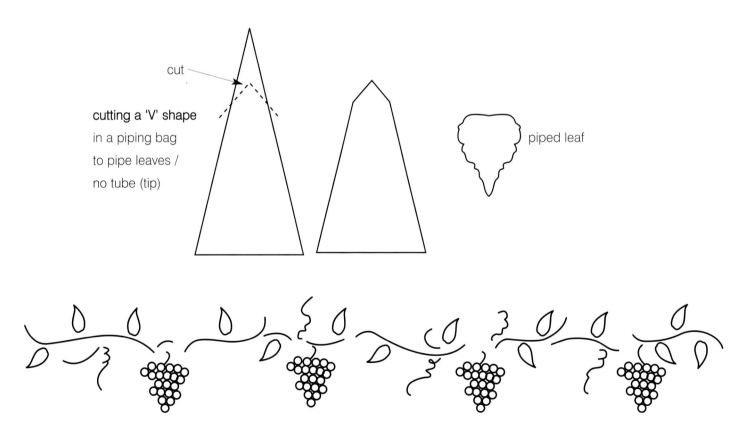

cut

cutting a 'V' shape
in a piping bag
to pipe leaves /
no tube (tip)

piped leaf

engagement celebration pages 102–104

floral cake pages 64–67

decorated tile cake / side design pages 76–79

decorated tile cake / side design pages 76–79

decorated tile cake / side design pages 76–79

decorated tile cake / side design pages 76–79

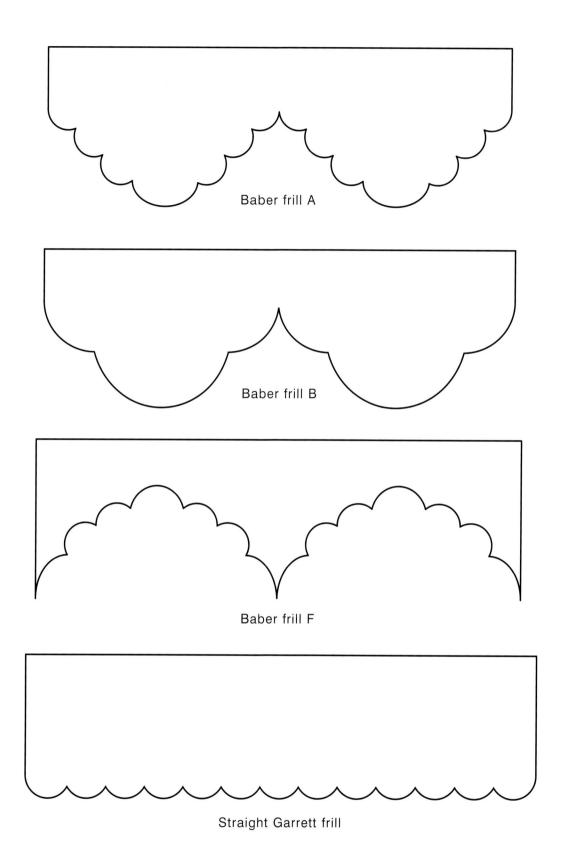

Baber frill A

Baber frill B

Baber frill F

Straight Garrett frill

broderie anglaise frills – can be drawn onto card,
cut out and used as patterns

suppliers

UNITED KINGDOM

Ann Baber (AB)
22 Lawrence Close
Worle
Weston-super-Mare
North Somerset
BS22 6TX

Ann Pickard (AP)
Flat 2, Edingworth
Mansions
2 Atlantic Road South
Weston-super-Mare
BS23 2DE

British Bakels
Granville Way
off Launton Road
Bicester, Oxon 0X6 0JT
Tel. 01869 247098
(Pettinice sugarpaste)

The Cake Corner
33 Orchard Street
Weston-super-Mare
Tel. 01934 626587

Ceefor Cakes
15 Nelson Road
Leighton Buzzard
Bedfordshire
LU7 8EE
Tel. 01525 375237

Cornish Cake Boards
Rose Hill
Goon Haven
Truro, TR4 9JT
Tel. 01872 572548

Culpitt Cake Art
Culpitt Ltd
Jubilee Industrial Estate
Ashington
Northumberland
NE63 8UQ
Tel. 01670 814 545

Edable Art (EA)
1 Stanhope Close
The Grange
Spenneymoor
Co. Durham, DL16 6LZ
Tel. 01388 816309

Guy Paul & Co. Ltd
Unit B4, Foundry Way
Little End Road
Eaton Socon
Cambridgeshire
PE19 3JH

JC Cake Supply Co.
Unit 6
Ivanhoe Industrial Estate
off Smisby Road
Ashby de la Zouche
Leicestershire, LE65 2UU
Tel. 01530 414554

Old Park Engineering
Co. Ltd
Teignmouth Road
Clevedon, Somerset
Tel. 01275 874004

Orchard Products (OP)
51 Hallyburton Road
Hove

East Sussex, BN3 7GP
Tel. 01273 419 418

P.M.E. Sugarcraft (PME)
Brember Road, Harrow
Middlesex, HA2 8UN
Tel. 020 8864 0888
www.pmeltd.co.uk

Polycones Co.
(Bolt Boxes)
17 Beach Green
Shoreham-by-Sea
West Sussex, BN43 5YG
Tel. 01273 454049

Squires Kitchen (SK)
3 Waverley Lane
Farnham
Surrey, GU9 8BB
Tel 01525 711749

Renshaw Scott Ltd (R)
Crown Street
Liverpool L8 7RF

Videopoint
Bothy Cottage
Kippens Lane
West Grinstead
West Sussex, RH13 8HY

AUSTRALIA

The Cake Decorating
Centre
32–34 King William Street
Adelaide 5000
Tel. +61 8 8410 1944

Cake Decorating School
of Australia
Shop 7
Port Phillip Arcade
232 Flinders Street
Melbourne
VIC 3000
Tel. +61 3 9654 5335
Fax. +61 3 9654 5818

Cake Ornament Co.
156 Alfred Street
Fortitude Valley
Brisbane
QLD 4006
Tel. +61 7 3252 5542

Cupid's Cake Decorations
2/90 Belford Street
Broadmeadow
NSW 2292
Tel. +61 2 4962 1884
Fax +61 2 4961 6594

GERMANY

Kopy Form Gmbh
Rudolf Diesel Strasse 1
D67259
Beindersheim

JAPAN

Sugar Dream
2/16 Shiroganedai
1/Chome
Minato/KU
Tokyo
Japan 108

NEW ZEALAND

John & Dianne Carruthers
46 George Street
Palmerston North
Tel.+64 6 357 9971

REPUBLIC OF IRELAND

Cakes and Co.
25 Rock Hill
Blackrock
Co. Dublin
Ireland
Tel. +353 1 283 6544

UNITED STATES

American Bakels Inc
8114 Scott Hamilton Drive
Little Rock AR 72209
Freephone: +1 1800 799 2253
Tel. +1 501 568 2253
Fax +1 501 568 3947
email: embakels@swbell.net
www.bakels.com

Beryl's Cakes Decorating
P.O. Box 1584
North Springfield
VA 22151 – 0584
Freephone: +1 800 488 2749

Fax. +1 703 750 3779
email: beryls@beryls.com
www.beryls.com

Cake & Baking Center
56 West 22nd Street
New York
NY 10010
Tel. +1 212 675 2253

Cake Depot
Suite #29, 7931 SW 40th Street
Miami
FL 33155
Tel. +1 786 388 9174

acknowledgements

I am deeply indebted to both Fiona Cowling and Nick Sparks, without whose help I would never have
been able to complete this book on time – Fiona with the cakes and Nick with his computer.
Many thanks to Caryl Peters of the Cake Corner, Weston-super-Mare, who was
a constant source of sound advice and constructive ideas.
To my friends Ann and Jean Pickard for their support and encouragement, as well as my Mum,
Sue Hills and Jean Martin, for their offer of help should it be needed.
Joe Astley of British Bakels, who so kindly negotiated the supply of Pettinice,
which is used in the decoration of most cakes in this book.
Tony Hole, photographer, not only the superb pictures, but for helping to ferry the cakes from my house to the studio.
P.M.E., for telling me about their new daisy cutters and sending a set for me to use on one of the cakes.
Steve and Joan Cornwell of Ceefor Cakes, for coping with my apparent inability to place an order correctly.
Beverly Dutton and staff of Squires Kitchen, for sharing their new product, chocolate marzipan,
and allowing me to use it in this book – also for the fresh supplies of folk art paints.
Colin Wheelock of Old Park Engineering, for making cutters at very short notice.
Margaret of Edable Art, for being so generous with anything I asked for.

index

First published in 2001 by Merehurst Ltd

Merehurst is a Murdoch Books (UK) imprint

Copyright © 2001 Merehurst Ltd

ISBN 1-85391-929 2

A catalogue record of this book is available from the British Library.

Commissioning Editor: Barbara Croxford

Project Editor: Carine Tracanelli

Designer: Maggie Aldred

Photographer: Tony Hole

Templates: Chris King

CEO: Robert Oerton

Publisher: Catie Ziller

Publishing Manager: Fia Fornari

Production Manager: Lucy Byrne

Group General Manager: Mark Smith

Colour separation by Colourscan, Singapore

Printed by Tien Wah Press, Singapore

Murdoch Books (UK) Ltd
Ferry House, 51–57 Lacy Road,
Putney, London SW15 1PR
Tel: +44 (0)20 8355 1480
Fax: +44 (0)20 8355 1499
Murdoch Books (UK) Ltd is a subsidiary
of Murdoch Magazines Pty Ltd

Murdoch Books®
Wharf 8/9, 23 Hickson Road,
Miller's Point, NSW 2000, Australia
Tel: +61 (0)2 4352 7025
Fax: +61 (0)2 4352 7026
Murdoch Books® is a trademark
of Murdoch Magazines Pty Ltd